GW00567474

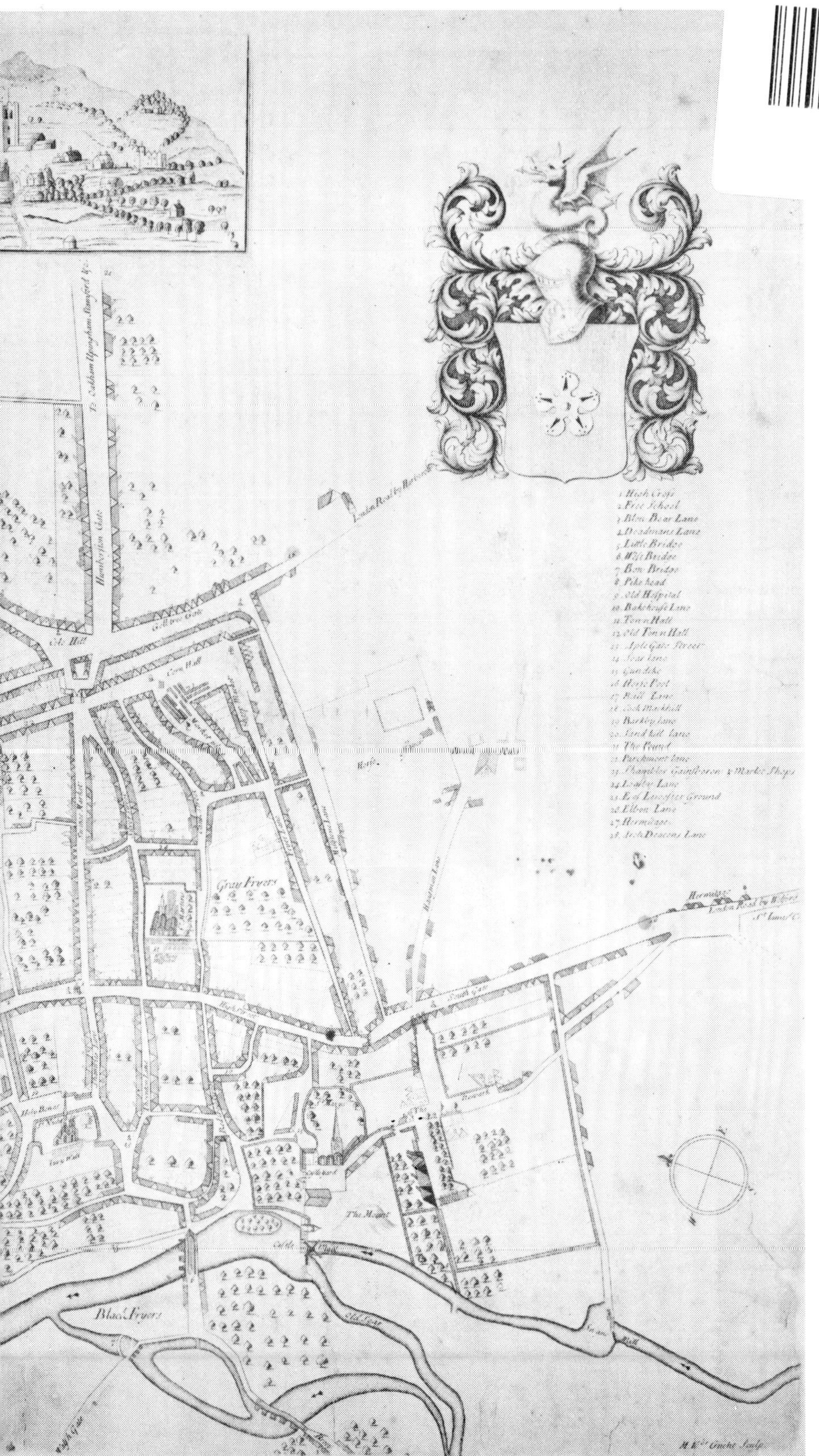
1 High Cross
2 Free School
3 Blue Boar Lane
4 Deadmans Lane
5 Little Bridge
6 West Bridge
7 Bow Bridge
8 Pike head
9 Old Hospital
10 Bakehouse Lane
11 Town Hall
12 Old Town Hall
13 Aple Gate Street
19 Barkby lane
21 The Pound
22 Parchment lane
24 Loseby Lane
26 Elbow Lane
27 Hermitage
28 Arch Deacons Lane
Grey Fryers
Black Fryers
South Gate
Hermitage
The Mount

Michael
SMITH

Co-op store dominated High Street in 1984

HERE'S a reminder of the days, not so long ago, when the central part of High Street was dominated the huge Co-operative department store, which sold everything imaginable and housed an enormous restaurant.

There were departments for all manner of things: men's and ladies' clothing, schoolwear, furnishings etc, as well as a food hall.

The road off to the side of the building is Union Street, which has disappeared in the development of the Shires and Highcross Leicester.

Its footprint is now one of the entrances to Highcross.

On the opposite side of Union Street, when this picture was taken in August 1984, was the Magnet Store, otherwise known as Arthur Whitcher's menswear shop.

The firm had been trading there since around 1902, when the store was built in place of the historic Huntingdon's Tower, which featured on this page recently.

go our athletes are training hard as they prepare to represent their country in what is being dubbed as the biggest year for British sport.

I've been working with the GB Rowing Team and helping to recruit participants for the "Nation on Trial" challenge. This event runs throughout February and is a great opportunity for everyone in the East Midlands to experience what the GB rowers go through as they battle for selection for the 2012 season.

A stroke can happen to anyone of any age. In the East Midlands around 9,700 people have a stroke every year. Take part in the "Nation on Trial" and you'll feel healthier, reduce your risk of having a stroke and help raise money for the Stroke Association. You could also win a behind-the-scenes day with me at the Olympic rowing venue.

"Nation on Trial" runs until February 29.

More information on the event, how to sign up and help with fund-raising can be found at:

www.nationontrial.org

Sir Matthew Pinsent.

CALL: Sir Matthew Pinsent – four times an Olympic gold medallist

Councillors need to engage more with residents

PETER Warzynski's excellent article "Parishes set out rises in tax bills" (Mercury, February 14) rightly highlights steep increases in some parish council precepts.

These hikes are often without mandate from the electorate.

In Blaby District, only two parish councils were contested at the last elections, Stoney Stanton and my own ward in Braunstone Town.

Seventeen of the 19 town councillors on Labour-controlled Braunstone Town Council, were untested at the ballot box.

Yet, they pushed through an increase of 2.5 per cent this year, making it one of the highest precepts in the county.

Contrast that with controlled budgets at Conservative-controlled Leicestershire County and Blaby District Councils.

At a time when residents' personal spending budgets are being squeezed, they are being handed down council tax increases, by parish politicians, who are untested at the ballot box.

Parish councillors really need to engage more with residents in the future – to legitimise any rises.

Councillor Ron Ward,
Braunstone Town councillor,
Thorpe Astley Ward (Con).

sickbay at the rapid diagnos mean we are working with partners, ens ledge at the u ness intellige

This year, as our £12.6 mill Centre at Gle many local or munities and Our research including dia transplant su fits for those i beyond where ics work and train build th

I am also par tion we make university's i at our Botanic visitors annu Leicester Con ival and there and exhibitio

As a major e economic imp regional econ pounds each ness and indu workforce for

I am particu status among ies which led without being University of university in stitutions to n inclusive.

The Univers origins throu and accessibi

■ *Professor Si of the Univers*

The Book of Leicester 1985
has been published
in a Limited Edition
of which this is

Number 287

A complete list of
subscribers is printed
at the back of the book

THE BOOK OF LEICESTER

FRONT COVER: Clock Tower before 1882. Immediately to its right the premises of John Burton, photographer.

The Cathedral steeple from Lower Brown Street; in the middle distance a Midland Fox bus passes up Newarke Street. With the exception of the Cathedral, built of stone, this part of Leicester – Lower Brown Street, Newarke Street, Marble Street, Chancery Street – is still largely brick.

THE BOOK OF LEICESTER

BY

RICHARD GILL

WITH PHOTOGRAPHS BY

CHRIS DOVE

BARRACUDA BOOKS LIMITED
BUCKINGHAM, ENGLAND
MCMLXXXV

PUBLISHED BY BARRACUDA BOOKS LIMITED
BUCKINGHAM, ENGLAND
AND PRINTED BY
LEICESTER PRINTERS LIMITED
LEICESTER, ENGLAND

BOUND BY
J W BRAITHWAITE & SON LIMITED
WOLVERHAMPTON, ENGLAND

LITHOGRAPHY BY
CAMERA-GRAPHIC LIMITED
AMERSHAM, ENGLAND

JACKET PRINTED BY
CHENEY & SONS LIMITED
BANBURY, OXON

DISPLAY TYPE SET IN BASKERVILLE
AND TEXT SET IN 11/12pt BASKERVILLE BY
GECKO LIMITED
BICESTER, OXON

ISBN 0 86023 218 2

Contents

Acknowledgements

I would like to thank a number of people who have helped me compile this book on the visual and architectural history of Leicester. Clive Birch both invited me to write it and guided me as to its contents. Kate Thompson and her splendid staff at the Leicestershire Records Office have both tolerated my inquiries and allowed me access to their collection of building plans. Most of the material in the last eight chapters has been gleaned from the work they have helped me to do there. At Newarke Houses Museum I have received a great deal of help from Jane Leggett and Sherri Brown. I am very grateful to Kirsty McClellan, who has worked on Clarendon Park.

Four other people, or groups, must be thanked. Because the visual character of Leicester is my main subject, I would like to thank all those people who have attended my evening classes at Vaughan College and Hinckley Road. I am sure that they will be able to see in the book many points which they have made to me. Chris Dove has taken many of the photographs. He has struggled against unpleasing street furniture to create images which, I hope, will make the citizens look again at their own City. Gillian Walters has done the typing. My wife, Mary, and my daughters, Miriam and Naomi, have not only put up with my disappearances – to my room, to the Records Office, or some obscure part of Leicester – but have also made a number of valuable points to me about the City in which we live.

For permission to reproduce a number of photographs I am grateful to the Leicestershire Museums, Art Galleries and Records Service. I am also grateful to Hodder and Stoughton for permission to print a passage from *Leicestershire* by W.G. Hoskins.

Solid, Victorian, brick-built and prosaic

Perhaps it is the city of Leicester of which the exile can say: This is the corner of the world above all others that has a smile for me. Solid, Victorian, brick-built and prosaic, Leicester has none of the dramatic quality of Nottingham with its great castle rock dominating the city, none of the character of the blackened-stone towns of the industrial North. It has no real centre, least of all—praise God— a civic centre in councillor's concrete. It has no street of any real distinction. No stranger would ever get excited about it. But it has a small town homeliness (for all its three hundred thousand people), a comfortable feeling of Sunday dinners and security, of chapels and libraries and much earnest winter reading and lecturing, of life still revolving around 'the old clock Tower' as it did in grandfather's time, that many of us find appealing and satisfying in a world that is increasingly buried in soulless concrete: a delightful Betjeman town that one would not willingly see too much changed.

W.G. Hoskins

Foreword

by Charles Phythian-Adams, Head of the Department of English Local History, The University of Leicester

Like its situation and its history, the personality of Leicester does not force itself on the attention; Leicester has to be lived to be undertstood. To appreciate its undemonstrative attraction, the City needs to be observed from within. Always a middling town; sited towards the geographical heart both of England and of its own shire; anciently crouched unobtrusively in the hollow of the Soar valley; and, as well as may be, evading some of the worst twists in our national history, Leicester has tended always to get on with its own business. Even in times of prosperity, it has aimed for comfort rather than urban grandeur. Few towns have so sucessfully hidden away from the prying eyes of strangers so fine a building as their new Town Hall of 1876. Even the street corners seem, at first sight, to receive more interesting architectural treatment than the sweep of the streets themselves.

Yet the personality of Leicester lies all around for those who are prepared to lift their eyes off the pavement and glance upwards above the modern shop fronts. It is a personality that was most strongly expressed before the advent of the modern tower-block, and especially during the piece-meal expansion of the period of 1880 to 1940 when the City engulfed some six neighbouring village centers and as many, more or less open, extra-parochial places. For all this multi-textured diversity, however, the place does have a sense of visual unity that derives largely from the warm colour-range of its almost universal brickwork – through from the modestly plain to the positively vibrant. And in looking at such matters, and much more besides, we could hardly ask for a more sensitive and knowledgeable guide than Richard Gill. With energy, enthusiasm and that discerning eye which perhaps only a friendly outsider may bring to bear objectively, he has something here to tell all of us who may think we already know the architectural secrets of Leicester. In particular, and without forcing it on our attention, he has consulted, as few before him have, the detailed documentation which is there to inform us accurately, not only about the timing of so many building developments, but also about those people, whether of national or of local repute, who were responsible for creating that quietly variegated environment which now is Leicester. This little book must be for every Leicester resident – there can be barely a street or a neighbourhood community which does not receive perceptive attention within its pages. For that, all of us should be grateful, since thereby all of us shall surely learn.

Dedication

For Mary, Miriam and Naomi, and
Eric Swift, who first showed me
that Leicester is interesting.

Introduction

This book traces the history of Leicester from Roman times to the present day; in other words, from Jewry Wall to Beaumont Leys. Such an undertaking is not unique. Several writers, some natives and others like myself who have chosen to come here, have tried to convey to Leicester people the variety, interest and character of this often neglected City of the East Midlands. To take up one's pen, then, needs the justification of a new perspective. This is why my book does not mainly deal with events or people. What stands at its heart is the City itself, as it is embodied in its buildings and layout. My aim is to relate its history by attending to what can be *seen*. This is why in most cases I deal with buildings that survive and why some centuries are more represented than others.

What follows is a not uncritical account of the City in which I have lived since 1966. I do find fault and I do have cause, on rather a lot of occasions, to regret what has been lost and to question what has gone on in some areas of our communal life. Yet I hope that the main spirit of this book is a celebratory one. I have always found Leicester interesting and the more I have learned of it the more I have found in myself a liking for this solid, red brick and cautiously progressive place. Indeed, I frequently find myself in the position of defending it against the frustrated accusations of its natives who sometimes find it no more than glumly provincial. Because I believe that Leicester is more than that, I am happy to take up its defence.

I had better add a comment about the photographs. Many of the buildings referred to in the text are also illustrated, but some are not. Also, there are some buildings and scenes which appear in photographs but are not mentioned in the text. It is, therefore, advisable to look upon text and photographs as two separate elements, which do and sometimes do not make reference to each other.

The Jewry Wall and the stocky tower of St Nicholas's Church – the most exciting piece of visual history in Leicester.

Ratae Coritanorum

The three major towns nearest to Leicester – Coventry, Northampton and Nottingham – have this in common: visual drama. The spires of Coventry, particularly from a distance, still present a distinctively medieval skyline; Northampton, when viewed from the south, seems to perch on the edge of a cliff, and Nottingham, the most dramatic townscape of the three, is dominated by its huge castle rock. Leicester is often thought to be quite different: here everything is visually unassuming, gentle, mild and engagingly domestic. Yet this view (one shared by both natives and newcomers) must admit to at least one exception: in the centre of the City there stand juxtaposed two buildings, the effect of which can only be called dramatic – the massive, weathered fragment of Roman work traditionally known as the Jewry Wall and, to the east and on higher ground, the impressively stocky form, tough looking and dark textured, of St Nicholas's Church. There can be few places in Britian where the past is so potently present.

Leicester's Roman past dates back to the establishment of a broad border region, dotted about with forts and served by the Fosse Way, running from Cirencester to Lincoln. The Romans were not the first inhabitants. The Coritani, a tribe that occupied Leicestershire, Rutland, Lincolnshire and Nottinghamshire, seem to have settled on the east bank of the river Soar. This large settlement (it may have stretched from the Newarke up to Great Central Station) owed its existence to the need for trade between peoples on the east and west sides of the river. That the river is easily crossed at this point is the geogrpahical condition without which Leicester could never have developed.

The Romans built at least two forts (river crossings can serve defence as well as trade) – one in Duns Lane and the other north of Elbow Lane, in the middle of the first century AD. Their presence no doubt stimulated further trade (paid soldiers spend money), and we may assume that when, about AD 80, they withdrew, the natives welcomed the establishment of their settlement as the *civitas* (regional capital) of the Coritani tribe. The road grid – a regular network of streets running north/south, east/west – was soon laid down, and shops, mostly built in wood, were erected. Tribes were not (could not be) forced to adopt a Roman way of life against their will, especially when they had to bear the cost of the building. This may explain why the Coritani concentrated for at least two generations on the building of shops. It was not till about AD 140 that public buildings appeared – the *Forum* (or market), the *Basilica* (the equivalent of the town hall) and the Baths. Mention of the Baths brings us back to Jewry Wall, but before we look at it in more detail something must be said about the name the Romans gave to Leicester – *Ratae Coritanorum*.

Coritanorum is easily explained: it means the place of the Coritani tribe. But what about *Ratae*? A popular view is that it is a Celtic word meaning ramparts or earthworks. If so, *Ratae Coritanorum* means: the ramparts of the Coritani people. There is an enticing speculation about how it got that name. To the north-west of Leicester there is a massive, rectangular earthwork of huge banks and deep ditches, which is called Ratby Bury Camp. It was once thought to be Roman because it has the playing card shape favoured by their military engineers, but recent thought (and some digging) suggests that it is late iron age. Ratby, because of its name ending, looks like a Danish name, but what if one concentrates on the first part. Could it be Celtic? If Ratby in Roman times was called something like *Ratae* it is difficult to believe that two settlements within about eight miles of each other should bear the same name. Perhaps, either by design or accident, the name of the camp was transferred to the settlement by the river Soar.

The great pile of masonry and the residual foundations that range from the wall to the west were the Baths of *Ratae Coritanorum*. The Romans placed the business of taking a bath at the centre of their social life. That baths were more than places of cleansing is clear from literature and archaeology. The impression Seneca creates is not a pleasant one: in his writing baths come over as a mixture of trendy keep-fit centres, holiday camps and rugby clubs. Archaeology, in the case of Leicester, adds the strong possibility that the baths adjoined a *palaestra* (an exercise or games hall). That being so, we may imagine the Jewry Wall as the grand entrance from the *palaestra* (on the site of St Nicholas's Church) to the baths. Originally it would probably have been plastered, painted and the niches filled with the statuettes of appropriate deities, including, no doubt, the goddess Fortuna.

Generations have found the Jewry Wall to be a mysterious thing; it has teased, and still teases questions from us. For years the major one was what was it? Stukely, who drew it in 1722, called it, following a medieval tradition, the Temple of Janus. Celia Fiennes, when she visited Leicester in 1698 after a tiring ride from Uppingham, reported that she saw 'a piece of Jury Wall as it's called being in arches and was a place where the Jews burnt their sacrifices'. Jack Simmons points out that as late as 1907 *The Victoria County History* was still calling it the west gate of the town.

And then there is the question of its name. There is no evidence of there being a Jewish quarter in the town, a point that has prompted the suggestion that the name is a corruption of Jurats – the senior members of the Corporation, twenty-four in number, who met in 'the town churchyard'. The suggestion is reasonable: there was a building that functioned as the town hall near St Nicholas's church.

The question, which I ask of any interesting building, is: who was the architect? While no name is likely to be found, it is worth considering what kind of a person he was. The style is Roman. It could have been built by a Roman architect or engineer from say, Lincoln. On the other hand, a Briton, even a native of *Ratae*, could have learned the art of Roman building and so designed it.

The question most often asked is: why has it survived? There are three possibilities: first, it is immensely strong. The principle that where your treasure is, there will your heart be, also applies to architecture: what a society most values it will build most strongly. Since baths were the centre of Roman life they were built to last. (An even more spectacular piece of Roman architecture – the great wall at Wroxeter – performed the same function as the Jewry Wall.) The second reason is closely related. The Wall has been stripped of useful building stone leaving only its core and, because the building was large, it is a massive one. Once the stripping of useful stone was over, it would have been both difficult and pointless to demolish the remainder. Thirdly, it has been advantageous to keep it. There is evidence of foundations connecting it to St Nicholas's Church; years later cottages were built on to it and, in the nineteenth century, it was incorporated into a factory.

There is one more point to make; it is personal though, I think, important: Jewry Wall is beautiful. In sunlight the colours of the brick and stone are to be relished – warm umbers, light sand, coal-grey lumps and something approaching terracotta or even orange. Its shapes and textures are pleasurable. To look at its gritty, ragged surfaces is to appreciate that exciting blend, so characteristic of weathered stone and brick walling, of the purposeful and the random: the stones have a function, yet their shapes, as in a dry stone wall, are pleasingly haphazard. In view of that, I am surprised it has not attracted more painters and print makers. Above all, there is beauty in its drama: thirty feet high, craggy in outline, built of six different stones in addition to brick, it rises above the foundations of the Baths with that air so characteristic of many ancient monuments – the assertion of solid persistency.

Of the rest of *Ratae Coritanorum* that remains visible, four features deserve attention. The first is probably related to the Jewry Wall. To the south of the City, just west of Aylestone Road, is a low, humped earthwork about a hundred yards long – the Raw Dykes. It stands on the 198 feet contour, one that continues as far as the Newarke, and this reinforces the suggestion that it was an aqueduct bearing water from the dammed Knighton Brook. Once in *Ratae*, engineers could have built a tower (remains of heavy masonry were found just south west of the Jewry Wall) to provide, by means of gravity, a constant water supply for the baths.

The second thing to notice are the marvellous remains in the Jewry Wall Museum. Some columns from the *Forum*, which lay under what is now the underpass (another is in St Nicholas's churchyard) stand by the entrance, while inside there are superb mosaic pavements (over thirty have been found in the City) and, perhaps most precious of all, some Roman plaster work. One section of this is in a rich crimson on which are painted some rather wonky architectural features. It comes from an opulent second century house which stood just north of the *Basilica* (near where the underpass emerges). The family either declined or, as sometimes happened, the house was cleared by the authorities to provide more market facilities. Then, as now, the shopping centre of Leicester was constantly shifting.

Of the streets, nothing remains on the Roman pattern apart from a section of Highcross Street as it passes All Saints Church and, possibly, the little street called All Saints Open. The interesting thing about *Ratae Coritanorum* was that it had a west/east axis, because the Fosse Way, entering at the West Gate (probably near the West Bridge) and leaving for Lincoln by the East Gate (near the Clock Tower), was the main road. It was not an axis that was to remain.

The final feature that deserves attention was the walls. Nothing remains above ground but their position, because the medieval walls followed them, controlled the shape of Leicester for centuries, and are still evident on to-day's maps. They ran just north of Horsefair Street, west of Granby Street, Gallowtree Gate and Churchgate and finally south of Sanvey Gate. It is likely there was a west wall. The differences in height between Talbot Lane and Bath Lane could be partly because Talbot Lane was built on the remains of such a wall. Elsewhere, there are discernible rises in the ground that indicate the presence of the town walls; there is a gradual rise from the Clock Tower up to Eastgate and the High Street and, even more noticeably, is the way a little alleyway (or Jetty) runs up from Sanvey Gate to Elbow Lane.

Ratae Coritanorum probably came to a quick end. Late in the fourth century there was a fire that swept through the *Forum* and the *Basilica*, after which nothing was re-built to original designs. Archaeological evidence suggests that rudimentary houses were later run-up in the ruins. Were they the houses of Britons or invading Saxons? If the latter, we may be sure that the Jewry Wall ceased to function as part of the Baths complex and began its subsequent life as something both useful and intriguing.

ABOVE: These remains are probably part of the colonnades from the Roman Forum, found in the St Nicholas Street area and re-erected beneath the canopy of the Jewry Wall Museum. BELOW: The remains of the Roman Baths west of the Jewry Wall were discovered when buildings were demolished in 1935 for swimming baths. Vaughan College, a sophisticated building which frames the site, designed by Trevor Dannatt in 1960, is the descendant of the Workingmen's College, founded not far away in Union Street in 1862 by Canon Vaughan, vicar of St Martin's.

Saxon, Dane and Norman

Jewry Wall is the result of one invasion; St Nicholas's Church to its east is, least in some of its parts, the fruit of another – that of the Saxons. There is no date for their arrival though, judging by burials such as those found in Churchgate, it could have been early in the sixth century. Nor is there a date for their conversion to Christianity. All we know is that Cuthwine, the first Bishop, was probably consecrated in 679. It is a mistake to think of St Nicholas's Church, as we now know it, as his Cathedral. The Church's exterior, with the possible exception of some work on the west wall, is entirely post-Conquest, and the Saxon work inside is too late, being in all probability tenth century – a date after the disastrous Danish invasions which, in the 870s, forced the Bishop to withdraw to Dorchester on Thames. But since a bishop must have his chair, his cathedra, somewhere, St Nicholas, if only because it stood near the centre of the Roman town, is as likely a site as any.

Of the Saxon work in St Nicholas, the north wall of the nave has a blunt presence. This is partly due to the unfortunate stripping of plaster that occurred in 1873 and 1874, an act which creates a general air of heaviness throughout the building. But what is most striking is the drama of the two great Saxon windows – huge, yawning gaps, haloed somewhat coarsely by two bands of Roman brick; a way of building which, like the materials, was probably picked up from the Jewry Wall. This wall was once the north wall of the church and not, as now, the division between the nave and a grim little north aisle. The north wall of the nave of St Nicholas is all that remains of the building between the departure of the Romans and the coming of the Normans, but there are three other lasting contributions from that period. The first is Leicester's name. The point can be simply put: Leicester is not called Ratchester. As early as the seventh century it was called *Legorensis Civitas*, a name the origins of which have been much, though inconclusively, disputed. Some say it was a river name, but then there is no evidence that the Soar was ever called anything else; others that it derives from a Welsh word meaning 'English', yet there is no satifactory reason why such a name was used; finally, it could derive from a personal name. The third possibility, if it is turned on its head, may explain Geoffrey of Monmouth's assertion that Leicester was founded by King Lear. What is more likely is that Geoffrey, or someone else, derived the name Lear from Leicester.

The second involves a speculation about a medieval suburb and street names. Although the Roman walls controlled the shape of Leicester for about fifteen hundred years, there was, by the Norman conquest, a large suburb centering on St Margaret's Church. Its origin could lie in the site of a Danish settlement. The invading Danes of the ninth century would hardly have wished to settle in the areas occupied by the Saxons; so did they move to the north-east? Certainly the streets leading up to and away from the Church bear the suffix 'gate': Churchgate, Sanvey Gate, Woodgate, Gallowtree Gate. 'Gate' here is Danish for 'way' or 'road'. There is, however, a difficulty: it looks as if the word passed into English speech, so these particular street names may date from a later period. What we now know as Guildhall Lane was called Kirk Lane in 1478, but Kirk Gate in 1483.

The third contribution is speech. Danish has affected the way we speak. The Leicester phrase 'mi duck' is probably derived from a Danish word meaning 'doll'. And what about the local habit of abbreviating long words to a di-syllabic form, ending in a 'y', which is usually pronouned in the back of the throat as an 'eh'? When we turn Victoria Park into Vicky Park and Skegness into Skeggy, we may well be practising an intonation inherited from the Danish invaders.

The effects of that invasion are ambiguous; those of the Norman are not. William, in his push from the south, came to Leicester in 1068 and probably built, or strengthened the Castle. By 1070 he had given it, together with the Lordship of Leicester, to Hugh de Grandmesnil. The Castle, therefore, should be seen as a sign of Norman power. Given its present state, this is not so easy. The Castle is a tranquil backwater reached from the north by a wonderfully picturesque gateway of black and white timbering and pleasingly weathered brick, and from the south by the ruins of the Turret gateway, one of the few bits of the Castle complex that accords with romantic ideas of what a castle should look like. The castle mound itself was levelled in the early years of the nineteenth century for the playing of bowls, and consequently appears to be no more than a pleasant hump which, in the spring and early summer, is lent a beguiling beauty by daffodils and Queen Anne's Lace. As for the hall itself, its function as a court means that it is usually only seen by the legal fraternity and their clients. Its exterior is a charming William and Mary brick facade, and inside it is divided into two courts, the furnishings of which are early nineteenth century.

Still, for those who wish to re-capture some sense of Norman power, there are a few sights to seek out. The Turret gateway is an impressive ruin, but even more striking is the great wall –whitish stone blotched with green lichens, regularly pierced with irregular holes, and capped with heavy, dressed stones – that runs from the gateway to form the southern limit of St Mary de Castro's graveyard. Even to-day, when we are used to tall buildings, it intimidates by its height and bulk. And although the mound is not high, it is still worth climbing its steep sides to enjoy views of the little brick cottages within the Castle grounds, the spire of St Mary de Castro and the great hall of the Castle. And at the base of the mound there is the crumbling entrance to John of Gaunt's cellar – great lumps of worn and pock-marked stone round an opening. Finally, if you can gain access to the Castle, look at the great beams supporting a roof, which is, according to Professor W. Horn, the oldest timber roof in Europe. The beams are massive, and I do not think it merely fanciful to find in them a purposefulness and drive which is quintessentially Norman.

The Normans added the stocky tower to St Nicholas's. From the sweeping St Nicholas Circle the clock tends to render the effect somewhat tame but, from the north – that is from Jewry Wall Street: it is, if you can ignore the quite horribly mechanical transept of 1889, a moodily dominating presence – hard, dark and boney. The west door of All Saints is also Norman.

But for Norman work at its grandest and, though the term is not often used of architecture of that date, at its most sumptuous, a visit to St Mary de Castro is essential. Here, as with the Castle, is an example of Norman swagger. It is, in fact, with the exception of the vanished Abbey, the nearest that Leicester got to the great Norman cathedrals and religious houses built as proud expressions of political and spiritual supremacy. The Church was founded in 1107 by Robert de Beaumont, third overlord and first Earl of Leicester, as a Collegiate Church for a dean and twelve canons. Much of the simple blank tracery and big openings to the west probably date from then. The Church's chief architectural glory, however, comes from the period of the second Earl, Robert le Bossu, or 'the hunchback'. He it was who founded the Abbey in 1143, built the great hall of the Castle in about 1150, and then, in the 1160s, was responsible for the lofty chancel of St Mary's which, when built, was higher – and certainly grander – than the nave. Building appears to have gone on for a couple of decades; the magnificent sedilia with its three rows of robust zig-zag work and its lively organic carving in the capitals of the twin shafts looks to date from around the 1280s. The chancel still looks and feels spacious. In an otherwise ominously dark church (the great gaping Norman openings on what is now the south wall of the nave look positively sinister), it is light (the large, high windows ensure that), airy, uplifting and elegant. Elegance, indeed, is still the key-note of St Mary's: it is one of the few Anglican churches in Leicester where one can escape the inanities of the *Alternative Service Book*!

Robert le Bossu's son, Robert Blanchesmains, had the exactly opposite effect upon the fabric of Leicester than that of his father. Le Bossu was a builder and founder; his son, albeit indirectly, brought destruction. But he started well. His wife, Petronilla, encouraged building work in the Abbey and (the kind of story which even if it is not true persists with mythic force) donated a hanging lamp suspended from the roof of the choir by a rope of her own hair. Then the Earl chose to take arms against Henry II. The King, in revenge, sacked Leicester in 1173, and in 1174 ordered the destruction of the town's, as well as the Castle's defences. The sack was mostly in the northern part of the town: the area north of the present day High Street and south of Sanvey Gate. It appears to have been savage. Some citizens left for towns as far away as Bury St Edmunds and St Albans. In a sense, that part of Leicester never fully recovered. Even to-day it feels deserted and looks neglected, as if it is only fit for factories, industrial units and monstrous 1960s ring roads. At one time there were five medieval churches in the area: All Saints, St Clements, St Leonard's, St Michael's and St Peter's. Now, only the sad, closed, redundant All Saints remains. All the others, although they might physically have survived the sack, owe their disappearance to the de-population it caused. St Clement's, which stood south of Soar Lane near to Jarvis Street, staggered on till at least 1536, when John Leland saw it, but shortly afterwards it must have been demolished. St Leonard's stood just beyond the north bridge on a site occupied by its recently demolished successor – a gaunt, brooding hulk built in 1876–1877 by Ordish and Traylen. It dated from the early thirteenth century and had entirely disappeared by the eighteenth. St Michael's stood in that rather lost area east of St Margaret's Baths. Although it continued in use after the sack, the parish declined, and the church was no longer in use by the fifteenth century. St Peter's, the grounds of which stretched from St Peter's Lane towards where the old Salem Chapel stood on Freeschool lane, was in use until the late sixteenth century, when its parish was united with All Saints.

LEFT: St Nicholas from the north: the solid (and much restored) crossing tower dominates the dark walls. RIGHT: The thin, needle-lke spire of St Mary de Castro was originally built in the early fourteenth century and reconstructed in 1785. BELOW: There is a much quoted remark from Professor Horn that the Great Hall of Leicester Castle is 'the oldest surviving aisled and bay divided hall of Europe', and that the roof is 'the earliest residential timber roof in Europe'. It is a pity the people of Leicester do not see it unless they are concerned with legal matters.

A Medieval Market

However hard life was after the sack, the town survived, for it was a centre for trade, as is evident in three aspects of medieval Leicester: the axis of the town, the streets and the importance of the markets.

Roman Leicester had existed on a west/east axis because of the Fosse Way but, during the middle ages, the military need to travel from Cirencester to Lincoln disappeared. Instead, the axis of the town became a north/south one, with what is now Highcross Street as the main thoroughfare. This change was no doubt due to a number of factors, principally economic. Leicester to-day hardly suggests the importance of Highcross Street; the medieval High Street of the town (that is what it was called) has dwindled into two stretches of road which, in spite of its designation as the A50, are of minor importance. A third remaining part has now been bogusly re-named Applegate. One section from Sanvey Gate to Burley's Way does retain a medieval feel with All Saints Church's west door opening directly onto the street. The other bit, although it contains the sadly mutilated Tudor grammar school, the entrance to what was once Blue Boar Lane, at the inn of which name Richard III slept before Bosworth and, set in the road, a cross to mark the site of the medieval market, simply appears to be a lost and scrappy one-way street.

In the centre of Leicester there are still a number of roads that are clearly medieval in origin; they bend and turn with a certain quirky charm. Cank Street, for instance, runs from St Martins, itself a medieval street, down to Cheapside, curving all the time so as rarely to disclose its full extent from one viewpoint; Silver Street gently deviates from a straight course, and Bond Street meanders slightly to the west from the point where it leaves High Street. Some are medieval but, because of demolition and modern pre-fabrication, have nothing redolently antique about them. St Peter's Lane and Causeway Lane are two such.

Markets were (and are) important for Leicester. The Wednesday Market was held around the Highcross at the junction of what is now High Street and Highcross Street, and the Saturday Market in the area we now know as the Market Place. Both were ancient, that of Wednesday dating back to the twelfth century, the Saturday one perhaps even earlier. Since the amalgamation of both in 1884 the contrast in the two sites is both striking and sad. One is loud, busy and extensive, while the other is indeed a scrappy one-way street. Even Humberstone Gate, where a fair was held till the early years of this century, has at least its breadth to suggest former use; Highcross Street has nothing but that cross in the road to indicate its former bustle. What that commemorates was a market cross which survived till 1577, when it was replaced by a secular looking octagonal structure with a cupola. This, in turn, decayed till, in the eighteenth century, only a few piers remained. One of these now stands in Cheapside as the centre-piece of a still rather raw and somewhat ponderous re-furbishment scheme – an ironic reminder of the demise of one market site and the continuing success of another.

The Market Place has about it that air of liveliness which helps to keep together tradition and the needs of the present. It has changed much. In the sixteenth century there were rickety stalls, shops and lean-tos, all doubtless of a crazy appearance; there was a great elm, beneath which pigeons were sold until the eighteenth century while, in the section running parallel to Gallowtree Gate, there stood the Corn Wall on which farmers showed off their livestock or displayed their grain. The central building has undergone considerable changes, from the late fifteenth century Gainsborough to the handsome Corn Exchange with, in front of it, Ordish's witty conceit – an almost Venetian archway. Yet for all this change there is a tangible feeling of continuity. The market still serves its original function and, in spite of the awful egg-box structure that serves as a not very attractive roof, the life that goes on beneath it is still that satisfying, open exchange of money and goods in which the purchasers feel they are buying bargains and freshness, and the vendors make pleasing profits. When the shopper passes through the dog-leg of Morley's Arcade (once the yard of the celebrated Angel Inn), or enters the market down those long passages (originally cuts through the town walls), from Gallowtree Gate, he or she would be justified in feeling a bond with generations who have trod those same paths bent on the same necessary purpose.

Many of the matters concerned with trade, as well as the general running of the town, were handled in the Guildhall. Originally it was the hall of the Corpus Christi guild, but so powerful did that body become that it merged with the Corporation itself. It is a marvellous building. It bulges and warps (too much for safety?) over the Lane, while its gables advertise its presence to anyone passing down Loseby Lane. The low and even secretive entrance opens into a visually crowded little square, which is flagged by huge slabs and overlooked by plastered surfaces, the white of which wonderfully sets off the slightly drunken and, on the ground floor, quite large window frames. There is also the surprise of height: the gabled staircase turret seeming to perch above the gables of the Mayor's parlour and the fourteenth century hall. This hall feels relaxed, open and communal – very much the sort of place in which to hold a feast. The great timber roof of attractively varied construction creates an atmosphere of security and good humoured confidence. Beneath it one feels one belongs. Up the staircase is the old library – great leather tomes, the very size of which seems to offer the prospect of erudition. The room, on the site of the living quarters of the chantry priests employed by the guild, is given special character by the irregular floor of massive timbers. From this room one can see the west end of St Martin's, in the south aisle of which the guild had its chapel.

Architecturally, St Martin's is almost entirely Victorian but its status as the 'town church' is due to its proximity to the Guildhall. It is a disappointing building. Were there a prize for the most uninspired cathedral in the United Kingdom, it would easily find a place on the shortlist. Inside it is dark without being mysterious; lacks, with the exception of the double south aisle, any spatial tension; is not, on the whole, improved by its twentieth century fittings; and, the most unattractive thing about it, smells strongly of wood and polish.

For medieval grandeur, other than that found at St Mary de Castro, one must turn to St Margaret's. The interior is disappointing, being rather hard and chilly, but the exterior is magnificent. The great west tower, visible from so many angles, is as noble in its assured perpendicular as many of the great Cotswold churches; the south porch, with its pinnacles, panelling, niches and gargoyles, is superb; and the big fifteenth century nave leads to a gloriously high chancel of the same period. One could be in a village near to say, Cirencester or Gloucester, yet all around are factories, and the air is rarely free of the sound of roaring traffic. This grandeur may be due to the fact that, unlike many other churches in the town, it belonged, not to Leicester Abbey, but to the Bishop of Lincoln.

There is, nevertheless, a rather sad link between St Margaret's and the Abbey: John Penny, one of the last Abbots of Leicester, was a native of the town who became Bishop of Bangor and then of Carlisle and, dying in 1520 on a visit to Leicester, he was buried in St Margaret's. His memorial still stands in the chancel. The contrast between St Margaret's and what remains of the Abbey is dramatic: the former, though no longer a great parochial church, is a fine building; the latter, apart from John Penny's great wall, is reduced to a crude set of re-constructed foundations in the bare and windswept northern section of Abbey Park. The pathos of the place is somehow sealed by the modern 'memorial', in the shape of a tomb, to Cardinal Wolsey which, exposed and lonely, bears the words: 'Give him a little earth for charity'. The forlorn scene (unusual in Leicester's parks) is enhanced by the connection for many Leicester people between Wolsey and, not the historical figure, but the knitwear firm, whose factory was built nearby. Hence the story of a restaurant chain, which advertised on a 'bus that their new premises would be called the Wolsey Tavern, and of the passenger who turned to her neighbour and said: 'Well, fancy that, naming a restaurant after a factory.'

Also to be swept away at the Reformation, though not with quite the same thoroughness that destroyed the Abbey, was the work in the Newarke. In the late medieval period it must have been a remarkable place: a walled citadel adjoining the Castle and encircled within it a hospital for the elderly, several houses for canons and chantry priests, and what was probably an exquisitely refined, though not large church. The whole ensemble grew gradually. It started in 1331 when the prematurely aging Earl Henry founded a hospital for fifty people, run by a warden, four chaplains and five nurses. His distinguished son Henry, the first Duke, expanded the hospital and in 1355 founded a church dedicated to the Annunciation. The chantry houses, including one for those who prayed for the soul of international merchant and generous benefactor, William Wyggston, came later. The Church was destroyed soon after the Reformation, the walls of the Newarke were breached when Prince Rupert laid seige to Leicester in the Civil War, but even as late as the early twentieth century its enclosed character persisted. The entrance was through the enormous, grey, fifteenth century Magazine Gateway.

There are few things in Leicester quite as sad as the treatment meted out to the Newarke. The gateway remains an incongrous monolith past which motor cars sweep from two directions into Newarke Street. It looks more than just forlorn – it is utterly out of place. The beautiful church, built to enshrine a holy thorn, is reduced to two arches in the basement of the Polytechnic. Approached past bits of electronic equipment and technicians in white coats, it is surrounded by a neatly laid out careers reading area, so that it has the oddity of one of those surrealistic pictures in which two quite unconnected images are juxtaposed to form a single picture. The chantry house of William Wyggeston happily survives as the western end of the Newarke Houses Museum and, best of all, the Trinity Hospital, with its dark chapel filled, possibly, with statues from the demolished church, lines the main road. There s also the fragment of another medieval house built into a factory on the corner of Gateway Street. But there is no sense of enclosure, and consequently, no sense that this was a place in which the highest in Leicester bestowed spiritual and physical care upon needy citizens.

OPPOSITE LEFT: The Castle Gateway of 1446 forms an attractive entrance to the enclosed courtyard of the Castle or, passing the other way, to the south door of St Mary de Castro. RIGHT: St Martin's, the 'town church', early 1870s, after Raphael Brandon had added the fine steeple, but before the Vaughan memorial porch was built. The remains in the foreground are the result of the demolition of Wyggeston's Hospital. BELOW: All Saints fronts the medieval High Street. In 1436 Margery Kempe was 'tried' there by an ecclesiastical court, because the Mayor thought her to be 'a false Lollard, and a false deceiver of the people'. The court was more understanding. ABOVE: St Margaret's Church soon after Sir George Gilbert Scott's restoration of 1862–1865. BELOW: A Victorian architect's view of Leicester's past: Joseph Goddard did this romantic drawing of the Blue Boar Inn, the hostelry where Richard III stayed before the Battle of Bosworth in 1485. The Blue Boar itself was demolished in 1838.

LEFT: There are two stories about the fate of Richard III, the most romantic of which is commemorated at West Bridge: the citizens of Leicester revenged themselves upon him at the Reformation by digging up his body and dumping it in the river here. The less technicolour version is that his bones still lie in the earth beneath Greyfriars. RIGHT: The spire of St Mary de Castro forms a splendid background to the athletic statue of Richard III, in Castle Gardens: the work of James Butler.

BELOW: A 1912 photograph of the Guildhall before Bedingfield and Grundy's restoration of 1922.

LEFT: Cottages on Bridge Street, typical of pre-red brick Leicester; to the right, the real Applegate, not the bogusly re-named section of Southgate; Pink was a dyer and Goodall a fruiterer. RIGHT: Old houses on Lower Red Cross Street: the building on the far left is the end of Parliament House, so-called because Parliament met there in 1414. BELOW: The early fifteenth century gateway to the Newarke (now known as the Magazine Gateway), from inside the Newarke, looking east towards Newarke Street.

John Flower's Leicester: a pre-red brick townscape of lath and plaster, peeling stucco, crooked gables, irregular roof-lines, shuttered windows and upper storeys perched precariously above squat, shadowed ground floors. Caught with that loving detail so characteristic of Flower is Shambles Lane, a vanished street roughly on the line of St Nicholas Circle, as it approaches the west end of High Street.

Timber and Brick

In 1920 Billson concluded his *Medieval Leicester* with a chapter on its destruction. Now while it is true that most of the medieval has gone, more of it survives than sixteenth, seventeenth, and some decades of eighteenth century Leicester.

The Reformation left Leicester poor and, if events such as the riding of the George (the first of the public games to go) had been popular, their suppression made it more cheerless. Morris and maypole went, and records of players visiting the town are few. Did the people turn to bear baiting, in which case where was the bear garden? The 1548 suppression of chantries must have increased poverty; from 1568 there were collections in church for the poor, and in 1587 a Royal commision on the fabric of houses that had once belonged to the guilds included phrases such as 'great decay', 'wholly wasted and utterly decayed' and 'the great gaps and ruins – yea even in the principal streets of this town'. To the general air of poverty and decay were added storm – 1563 – and pestilence – 1564, 1593–1594, 1609–1611. The town did not grow.

As to what it looked like we have to rely on John Flower. In the 1820s he executed a series of water colours, which depict a town of patched and peeling lath and plaster houses with crooked gables, leaning walls and tiny windows. Flower may have realised that he was capturing the last few years of a townscape which would probably disappear. There certainly seems to be implicit in his style the attitude of somebody both relishing, and lovingly recording the visual texture of what was doomed. Of the post-reformation town that Flower recorded little remains. The shop that adjoined the gaol in Highcross Street is still there, though that is more likely to be seventeenth or eighteenth century and, of course, the Guildhall survives. In addition there are three other remnants. They may all be pre-reformation; nevertheless, they are the nearest we can get to what Tudor, Stuart and even later Leicester was like.

One is a bit of timbering at the back of a house adjoining All Saints on Highcross Street. What is visible is a small gable end. The second is very much larger and also puzzling: there is a big timber framed building hidden behind shops on the south side of Silver Street. At present much of it is clad in later brick, but on the gable end the timbers are visible. Was it a large house or could it have been another guildhall? The third is the Costume Museum, traditionally known as Roger Wigston's house. It is a big timber framed building placed at right angles to the part of Highcross Street which has been re-named Applegate. On the ground floor there is a rhythmical pattern of windows between wooden mullions and, in the over-sailing first floor, a fine queen-post roof. It probably dates from around 1480 and is associated with Roger Wigston, on the grounds that the initials 'R.W.' apear in a wonderful set of stained glass windows that were formerly in the house, but are now on display in the Jewry and Newarke Houses Museums.

Of seventeenth century houses only two survive: Skeffington House and the ruinous Cavendish House in the north east corner of Abbey Park. The broad front of Skeffington House (the central section of Newarke Houses Museum) has three gables and regularly spaced stone windows with Tudor style hood moulds. It has been much restored but is thought to date from about 1600. It looks prosperous, an effect enhanced by the tall rusticated gate piers, and has about it an air of comfortable secularity. The secularity of Cavendish House is even more evident. Built, it is said, out of the remains of the Abbey in about 1600, it must have been substantial: on its first floor six mullioned and transomed windows and on the ground floor a big doorway. It was fired in 1645 after the siege of Leicester.

Only two other buildings, or parts of buildings, survive from the sixteenth and seventeenth centuries. One is the grammar school. This is characteristically Tudor: a free school built in 1573 out of the stones of St Peter's Church. That it was stone built and was given a fine Swithland slate roof is a token of the importance laid on education, and the esteem with which the benefactors felt their public charity should be regarded. As an institution its long history came to an end in the 1830s when, owing to the premature senility of a headmaster who refused to retire, it collapsed. The money that maintained it was used to pay for the education of boys at private schools till, in the 1890s, it was placed at the disposal of the Wyggeston Schools. The fate of the building is an unhappy one. Used for many years as Spurway's carpet warhouse, it was 'restored' in the 1960s so brutally that it lost its dormers and original windows; indeed, since nothing remains but the stone and slate, one wonders whether preservation was worthwhile.

It is a relief to turn to the Mayor's parlour in the Guildhall. The room dates from 1563 and the present furnishings – the rich, dark panelling, the Mayor's seat, and the wonderful fireplace – are of 1637. The room has a close, conspiratorial atmosphere, an effect in harmony with the smug, self-perpetuating Corporation that met there to do their – and the town's – business. In the smell of the wood one can almost detect the power, the complacency and the corruption.

Deals of an economic kind were what Leicester existed on in those years. The markets were busy and numerous. In addition to the Wednesday and Saturday markets, there were markets in Applegate and Redcross Street for meat, in Woodgate for timber, in Horsefair Street for cattle, sheep and horses and, on the site of the Clock Tower, the Haymarket. But between 1670 and 1680 an important economic change occurred: tradition has it that Nicholas Alsop introduced the stocking frame. Henceforth Leicester became a place of industry as well as of trade. The stocking frame, however, did not have the visual impact made by the market; since the industry was entirely domestic, no special buildings were necessary.

What did make a visual impact was brick. The transformation of Leicester from a lath and plaster town to one of red brick took a long time and was not complete until a few decades into the twentieth century, when all the other buildings had gone, and concrete had not yet been introduced. What is clear is that for many years it was used for some of Leicester's larger buildings. John Flower's work shows the persistence of the older material, but he cannot be taken as evidence that brick was not extensively used; after all, it was lath and plaster in which he was interested, not brick.

The first important use of brick was the front added to the Castle in 1695. A few years later, in 1708, the Great Meeting Chapel and school building were erected. With the benefit of hindsight, that is appropriate: Great Meeting was to dominate Leicester's political life, particularly in the nineteenth century, so it is fitting that the materials of that period should have been used. Although it has been much restored and altered (always a sign of a thriving organisation), it remains in its own plain and solid way an evocative building. Rather sombre outside, it has a high, light interior, a nice plaster ceiling of 1786 and some good memorials. Even better are the sober grey headstones that line the gardenlike chapel grounds. What is more difficult to realise now is its former power and influence. Its melancholic atmosphere of departed glory is most easily registered on a dark November day: the bulky forms of chapel and school, the tall presence of the wooden warehouse on Churchgate, and the lines of slate headstones seem palpable in contrast to the spindly shapes of the drooping trees and, nearby, the busy life of a large cash and carry store.

Another piece of eighteenth century brickwork was the cladding of the Lord's Place tower in High Street. This building, which survived till 1900, was built in the late sixteenth century as the town house of the third Earl of Huntingdon. As such it stands with Skeffington and Cavendish Houses, but it has been mentioned here because the addition of brick shows that by the eighteenth century it was thought appropriate to have a big building in that material. Lord's Place was not the only example in Leicester. The attractive Georgian house which forms part of Gateway College is dated 1772, and the attractive front added to Roger Wigston's house, usually known as 18 Highcross Street, must be of a similar date. In the outlying villages, now absorbed by the City, big brick houses were built: Belgrave Hall in 1713, Knighton Hall not much later, and Belgrave House and Braunstone Hall in 1776.

The finest eighteenth century brick buildings are all found in the vicinity of St Martin's. It is possible to take a walk from north to south of the Church, keeping eighteenth century buildings in sight most of the time. If one starts at the corner of Loseby Lane (one of our least spoiled streets) and Guildhall Lane, there are big brick houses, hardly noticed by the passer-by because their ground floors have become shops. In Guildhall Lane itself there is a handsome three-storeyed house with string courses, quoins and big keystones, and a humbler one, now white-washed. A left turn into St Martin's Lane east takes one past eighteenth century fronts with good doorways (one with cherubs and swags), and a porch with fluted columns. The narrow thoroughfare is made atmospheric by setts in the causeway, sudden glimpses of secluded gardens, and the dark presence of the Cathedral's east end. In the street called St Martin's there is a spendid house, No 21, to the east and, on the south side facing the Cathedral, some more eighteenth century houses. From here New Street is delightful, particularly at the slight bend where eighteenth century work is on either hand. New Street, so named according to one tradition because it was a new street of brick houses, must date from the middle of the century when the big Greyfriars estate was broken up. Of the same date are some of the houses on Friar Lane. There is a good one in chequer brick on the corner with New Street, and then, to the east, some brick and rendered fronts lead up to No 17 – the finest of all: three storeys, seven bays, quoins, a pediment, keystones reaching to a stone string course, a feature that always makes for visual firmness and, in the centre, a big Venetian window. To complete the eighteenth century walk, turn into Millstone Lane where, on the north side, are some nice, essentially humble houses, which must date from the end of the century.

A prominent non-domestic brick building is the 1768–1771 core of the Royal Infirmary. With over two hundred years of building it is surprising that the original is so easy to find. Built as the result of a public subscription scheme organised by Dr William Watts, this big, purposeful building, the work of Benjamin Wyatt, can be located by going through the gate at the southern end of the hospital complex. Now flanked by later, and duller buildings, it yet remains possible to appreciate how impressive it must have been when it stood alone in open fields.

Benjamin Wyatt was not a local architect. Had Watts wanted a local architect, one was available – John Johnson. Along with Sir William Wilson and the two John Wings, Johnson is the most celebrated architect to have been born in Leicester before the nineteenth century. Though most of his work was done in London and Essex, he made a lasting contribution to his native city in the County Rooms, built in 1792 as a hotel but later functioning as assembly rooms, and after that in 1817 as the judge's lodgings. Modern building has blinded us to the subtleties of scale, yet even to-day it is still possible to appreciate the size of the building and consequently imagine the impact it must have had. It is stone-faced, has a rusticated ground floor, a porch with columns and, on the first floor, three huge windows, bas reliefs and two figures in shallow niches. Inside the first floor is an elegant ballroom with restrained plaster decoration. Johnson wanted to add a Brunswick Square, which would have been south of the town on the site of the Town Hall. That plan came to nothing, but he did build for his family the Consanguinitarium, a crenellated building with gothick ground floor windows which survived in Southgates till the 1920s. Also to be demolished were the Borough Gaol in Highcross Street, only a scrap of which remains, and a theatre. Contemporary with Johnson's work is Spa Place in Humberstone Road; it has scale, charm and presence.

The buildings of the 1790s indicate that Leicester was changing: there were assembly rooms in the old Corn Exchange and on the site of the Clock Tower; the first big factory, Donisthorpe's by the river Soar, was built in the last decades of the century and, perhaps most significantly, transport developed. The narrowness of the town gates, not demolished till 1774, forced north/south traffic to use Gallowtree Gate as the main thoroughfare so, when in 1768 the Manchester – London coach service began, the inns that served it were all in that vicinity: the Three Cranes and the Three Crowns. The population had grown though, due to multi-occupation, the town hardly extended beyond its medieval boundaries. Nevertheless, all the factors for growth were present: industry, transport and a readily available building material.

Highcross Street: on the right, the Tudor Grammar School. Spurway, a carpet dealer, took it over in the early part of the century. Note the hood moulds on the windows, the plaques recording the benefactors and the attractive row of hipped gables, which were brutally removed when the building was 'restored'.

ABOVE: The Mayor's Parlour: the panelling, sumptuous fireplace and the Mayor's chair with the fine coat of arms all date from 1637. The elaborate gas lights add to the atmosphere of power and complacency. BELOW: The Newarke Houses Museum is really three houses: left is the late medieval house built for the chantry priests, who prayed for the soul of William Wyggeston; centre is Skeffington House, a town mansion of about 1600; right is a jolly extension, complete with crenellations and Tudor windows, built about 1800. It now houses the Museum of Leicestershire life.

ABOVE: This 1866 photograph shows the ivy-clad remains of Cavendish House in Abbey Park, probably built from the remains of Leicester Abbey. It was fired in 1645 after the seige of Leicester. The Victorian cold frames have, unfortunately, gone. BELOW: The Newarke Wall in 1886: the series of patched up holes were originally openings for cannons during the 1645 seige of Leicester by Prince Rupert. Behind is Bonner's Lane, a thoroughfare named after the appalling Bishop Bonner, a notorious burner of protestants, and archdeacon of Leicester. OPPOSITE ABOVE: A photograph by Burton of the Market Place on a Saturday with the whimsical 'Bridge of Sighs' in front of the Corn Exchange, the statue of the Duke of Rutland, and (centre of the shops) the splendid (and now demolished) No 38, built by Shenton and Baker in 1880. LEFT: For years the water supply for central Leicester came down in conduits from the Highfields area, hence Conduit Street, to the Market Place and was supplied from a brick fountain. The conduit was taken down in the nineteenth century and re-built in Wigston, it decayed and was eventually demolished to make way for a school. RIGHT: The Queen Anne front of the Great Hall, from the top of the Castle Mound, was Leicester's first substantial building in brick. The Castle Mound was levelled to form a Bowling Green in 1804.

REGENT HOUSE

Great Meeting Chapel: built in the Butts in 1708 four years after the Presbyterians and Congregationalists united, it became a Unitarian chapel during the long ministry of Rev Charles Berry (1803 – 1859). Important Victorian members were: the Biggs brothers, Fielding Johnson, Samuel Stone and Josiah Gimson, who owned the Vulcan engineering works. LEFT: New Street was built when the Herrick estate, the site of Greyfriars, was broken up. On the right is No 11; on the left there stands the only surviving pump in Leicester. RIGHT: An eighteenth century street scene: on the right is Leicester's most lavish eighteenth century house – 17 Friar Lane, also known as Dr Benfield's. Beyond are more sober houses, now used as offices, in stucco and brick.

LEFT: St Martin's East, a narrow walk to the east of the Cathedral, is the nearest Leicester comes to having an enclosed area around the chief church of the diocese. Behind the mechanical rows of Swithland slate headstones stand eighteenth century houses: No 3A with a lead front added in 1904 by Everard and Pick, and Nos 5 and 7. RIGHT: All that remains of Leicester's town gaol is this section of walling on Highcross Street between a little sweet shop and an early twentieth century factory. Here Daniel Lambert – England's heaviest man – was gaoler, till he became too fat to squeeze down the gaol's narrow passages. BELOW: The Royal Infirmary probably in the 1860s or '70s. In the background is the original block by Benjamin Wyatt, and to the left and right the 1860s additions by Parsons and Dain.

ABOVE: John Johnson's local masterpiece: the County Rooms, built as a Hotel (hence Hotel Street) in 1792.
BELOW: Southgates in 1922 shows the Ellis memorial wing, built to enlarge the science facilities of Wyggeston Boys' in 1882, and to the right the plain frontage of John Johnson's Consanguinitarium, built in 1792.

The Age of Elegance

The one exception to the essentially medieval shape of Leicester was an area to the north east of the town around Belgrave Gate. The presence of the canal, which reached Leicester in 1794, encouraged industrial and residential growth around Navigation Street. In 1811 growth also became possible to the south.The Corporation had agreed with the Freemen in 1804 that, in exchange for grazing rights on what became Freemen's Common, the great South Field could be enclosed. This agreement was ratified in 1811, and streets were soon laid out: King Street between 1811 and 1813, Wellington Street in 1812 and Princess Road in 1815. By the late 1820s Regent Road, Rawson Street, Hastings Street, West Street, Tower Street (originally called Grosvenor Street) and Lancaster Road (originally called Cavalry Road) had been added. Newtown Street followed soon after. This development was different from that around Belgrave Gate because, at least in the laying out of streets, it was rapid, and because it almost entirely consisted of middle-class housing.

On the eastern edge of the South Field ran New Walk. Its character is indivisible from the factors that shaped its growth. Laid out in 1785 as Queen's Walk, it was for almost forty years a rural promenade, specially planted with shrubs and trees, from the town centre to the race course on Victoria Park. The views must have been attractive: to the east a few windmills and the upland area we now know as Highfields, and to the west gently sloping ground and the solitary, classical presence of the Royal Infirmary. One of the remarkable things about New Walk is that it remained a pedestrian thoroughfare. This is due to the Corporation who, in 1824, laid it down that New Walk should be 'for the purpose only of a footpath . . .'. Carriages were only allowed to approach houses from the rear; hence the back entrances from London Road.

Another important aspect was also settled in 1824 – its spaciousness. Building was allowed only on condition that houses were at least ten yards from the causeway. Thus New Walk is not, as it might have been, a narrow, oppressive tunnel; it is open, relaxed and induces a feel of unhurried leisure in its users. Spaciousness, almost paradoxically, goes hand in hand with another quality – intimacy. The mature, over-arching trees, together with stretches of grass in front of the set-back houses, create a spacious intimacy which is New Walk's special ambience.

The final factor shaping New Walk is its architecture. The first buildings were probably erected in 1825, and their style, not surprisingly, was a modest Regency classicism: brick rendered with stucco, pilasters, parapets, some Greek detailing, cast iron balconies and small-paned windows symmetrically placed. The earliest surviving houses are to be found on the eastern side (nearest to London Road); there are four opposite the Museum, a handsome Greek pair nearer to town and, next to them, a plain three-storeyed house with a biggish porch and a blank window. By 1844 a number of houses had been added but they, interestingly, still adhered to the Regency manner. Of these later ones the small pair with neat quoins and beautiful segmental bays is the best, and the three-storeyed block next to them the most striking. (These are on the west side.) Further south, beyond the railway which came in 1840, there is a terrace which is not stuccoed, but its style – parapet, pilasters and porches with columns – is the same plain and, in its grey brick, even severe classicism of the earlier houses. Also in the classical manner is the Museum, built in 1836 by Joseph Hansom as the non-conformist proprietary school. Its hunky Tuscan columns and massive, plain entablature and pediment make it the only 'heroic' piece of architecture in the Walk.

That such a style should persist in an unimportant town is not surprising. What is noteable, however, is that the 1830s and 1840s did not see an end to the spirit of Regency classicism; in New Walk there are buildings of the 1850s and 1860s, which are essentially in the same tradition as those of the 1820s. In 1852 Flint and Wickes built a terrace of five houses in Museum (originally Victoria) Square. They used light grey brick for a symmetrical composition with quoins and, above the first floor windows, some rather heavy segmental and triangular pediments. In 1852 they built a terrace of six houses opposite where Holy Cross now stands. These houses are similar to the ones in the Square, though marred by a ponderous rusticated porch. Between 1862 and 1865 William Rushin built fourteen houses on the eastern side of the southern section of the Walk. Although in red brick, the understanding behind them is still basically classical. Finally in 1867 three architects made contributions: W.S. Burton built three houses virtually indistinguishable from Rushin's; next door Shenton and Baker built a taller house in the same style, and James Frank Smith added a sympathetic block that ran from New Walk round the corner into University Road, finishing at the Park Hotel on London Road.

The subsequent architectural history of the Walk is patchier, both in consistency and quality of design. In 1878 Shenton and Baker built Nos 2 and 4: small, three-storeyed semis in brick with small-paned vernacular windows and, in the gables, semi-circular headed windows, which are vaguely reminiscent of Philip Webb's work. Upper New Walk with its forest of timber gables, delightful porches, hanging tiles, small panes and, at the corner of Salisbury Avenue, a turret, is an area with its own consistent style, albeit one markedly different from the rest of New Walk. The twentieth century has been unsympathetic and, at its worst, positively hostile. Holy Cross with is neo-perpendicular nave built as late as 1956–1958 is bland and out of place, but its contribution is almost benign compared to what happened in the '60s. Then a whole terrace of the earliest work was swept away to be replaced by a building which in every way is hideously inappropriate. Waterloo Way necessitated the demolition of Waterloo House, and to the south a lumpy office block was allowed. Fortunately, things stopped there, and subsequent work has been concerned with conservation.

The stylistic conservatism of New Walk is not unique in Leicester. In the streets of Southfields a similar, though not as dramatic pattern is evident. The terrace of stuccoed houses on Upper King Street is in the New Walk manner, and probably dates from the 1820s. It is a plain building apart from the little bits of decoration on the pilasters. Of a similar period is the sweeping, tall and imposing Crescent. It has been dated to 1826 and, unlike many other buildings in the area, its architect, William Firmadge, has been identified. Across the road from the Crescent are the delightful Crescent Cottages of 1836, surely the work of William Flint.

The same style is evident in buildings of the 1840s. The big houses that now form the Fielding Johnson Hospital date from before 1844, as does the distinctly rural and considerably humbler little terrace opposite. But the most impressive stylistic survival (or deliberate continuation?) is Newtown Street. It is not on the 1828 map, so the almost purely eighteenth century house on its southern side must be 1830s or even 1840s. In 1855 a brick terrace of eight houses on the corner of Newtown Street and Tower Street confirms the survival of a classical style. In 1864 C.W. Herbert was building in a similar manner in West Street and Lower West Street, and four years later he built the rather handsome houses in Regent Street with little balusters in the parapets.

It is worthwhile asking why such conservatism prevailed. There is no simple answer. An effort to maintain visual continuity must be an important motive in New Walk and Southfields. Nor must it be forgotten that these were *houses*: most people will tolerate architectural experiment in public buildings, but prefer the familiar at home. Thirdly, what is here called classicism is not, in its provincial forms, much different from the Italian style that was so popular, at least in Leicester, until the 1870s and 1880s. One can speculate that the modest and cautious spirit of the place is reflected in its choice of traditional styles. Some people find that kind of explanation attractive, but it is one that is difficult to prove or disprove. It is safer to suggest that a builder such as Herbert was already on the elderly side and so was more inclined to the traditional.

Unfortunately, the names of many of the architects of New Walk and Southfields are lost, but in another area of Leicester life – large public works – there is one name that dominates: William Parsons. He was born in 1796, articled to Firmadge and became County Surveyor in 1823. His large buildings included the Welford Road Gaol of 1825–1828, St George's Church of 1827, the County Asylum (now the University) of 1837, and the 1840 Campbell Street Station for the Midland Railway.

Leicester citizens must have found the Gaol an astonishing building. It is built in the manner of an Edward I castle with a huge gateway, portcullis and four crenellated towers. The great red brick walls that dominate Tower Street, Newtown Street and the recreation ground have that overwhelming sense of power, massiveness and height that in aesthetic circles of the time was called 'the sublime'. Indeed, nowadays the walls are more impressive in their style-less power than the historical games Parsons played with the baronial gateway. St George's, the first Anglican church built in Leicester since the Reformation, is a typical commissioner's church with a centrally placed west tower, smooth stone walls and gothic decoration that is hardly organic. Though urban, its setting in a tree-shadowed churchyard is redolent of most people's idea of the rural parish church. The Asylum is plain, classical and unfussy. Some of the side sections are, in Pevsner's words, 'grim though not undignified', but the main elevation is impressive without being forbidding. It is a pity that nothing remains of the Campbell Street Station, because the photographs of it show it to have been a masterpiece of the railway age, in the same family, stylistically speaking, as Euston and Newcastle. It was a temple to travel, finer in its proportions and details than Trubshaw's London Road station, which replaced it in 1892.

Another local architect of the early decades was William Flint. He was clerk of works for Parsons in the building of St George's, though he was in private practice by 1826. He built churches, warehouses, houses, bridges and factories. Many have been demolished, including the Jacobean workhouse in Sparkenhoe Street and the Greek News Reading Room of 1838. Of his remaining buildings, four are important: Whitmore's Mill of 1844, Charles Street Baptist Chapel of 1830, the New Hall (now City Lending Library) of 1831 and the Phoenix Building in Welford Place of 1842.

The Mill is perhaps the finest: a big brick box of classical proportions with a delicate row of dormer windows relieving the severe rhythm of small windows. Like the other early industrial buildings, it overlooks the Soar. Charles Street Baptist, along with the sedately grand Bishop Street Methodist Chapel of 1815, is the best piece of early nineteenth century non-conformist architecture. This appealing building, set back from the road behind attractive railings and a screen of trees, has an inviting porch, flanked by Doric columns, and some reticent Greek detailing on its stuccoed facade. The Baptists were a powerful group, but of their town centre chapels only this remains. The others – Belvoir Street, Friar Lane, Archdeacon Lane and Harvey Lane – are, with the exception of the first, demolished, the congregations, in most cases, having moved to new buildings in the suburbs. Historically speaking, the New Hall is interesting. It was built for the Liberals in the days when they had no political power, though after 1835 they effectively ruled the town for the rest of the century. Its style is Greek: solid massing of the elements, and decoration which is plain and even austere. Such plainness characterised liberal economic policies; after the profligacy of the old Corporation they were sparing and frugal. No more than fifty yards away is the Phoenix Building. Built as the house and office of Samuel Stone, Clerk to the Council from 1835 to 1872, and author of the internationally used *Stone's Justice Manual*, it is also Greek revival in style, though the fluted ionic columns that flank the central entrance make it less severe than the New Hall.

These houses on New Walk are opposite the Museum; they were built between 1825 and 1828 and have recently been restored.

LEFT: This pair of houses was amongst the first to be built in New Walk. In 1825 John Bankart sold his land for building, and by 1828 a number of houses appeared on the east side south of the Roman Catholic Church. RIGHT: This attractive grey brick terrace was built in New Walk before 1844. The big bay windows are not original. They were 'all the rage' in the Leicester of the 1870s, so many buildings were 'enhanced' by them. BELOW: This three storeyed block was probably built on the west side of New Walk in the late 1840s or early 1850s.

ABOVE: New Walk from the corner of De Montfort Street, looking south. The houses were all built by William Rushin from 1865 onwards. Though in brick they are still roughly in the classical manner. LEFT: The Museum has an interesting history. It was built by a Roman Catholic architect, Joseph Hansom (inventor of the Hansom Cab) as the nonconformist Proprietary School in 1836, in confident classicism. It became the Museum in 1849. RIGHT: Upper New Walk has many of the qualities of New Walk – the gentle rise towards Victoria Park, the slight bends and the mature trees – but the houses are English, not classical. Stockdale Harrison was responsible for the energetic terrace that ends with the turret on the corner of Salisbury Avenue.

ABOVE: Crescent cottages, dated 1836: this small end house of a terrace, built in brick, rendered with stucco, stands on the junction of King Street and Regent Road. The gentle classical manner persisted in Southfields. The building is popularly attributed to William Flint. BELOW: King Street and the Crescent is one of the few examples in Leicester of Regency buildings facing each other across the road. The stuccoed cottages on the right are a continuation of Crescent Cottages (1836) while the gentle sweep of the Crescent, the work of William Firmadge, dates from 1826.

LEFT: These stuccoed buildings in Upper King Street date from before 1844. Like a number of others in Southfields they are constructed in brick, rendered and provided with a little decoration. RIGHT: This big house on Newtown Street illustrates two important aspects of the Southfields development: it is conservative in style, for though it was probably built in the early 1840s it could have been designed forty or even fifty years before. The second is its size. BELOW: The stylistic conservatism of the Southfields development can be seen in this charming little terrace at the corner of Tower and Newtown Street. The classical mouldings, particularly those on the facing wall, could have been in use in the 1820s; in fact, this terrace was built by William Herbert in 1855.

ABOVE: When it was built on the outskirts of the town in 1825 the gaol must have been unusually impressive because of its size and the 'romantic' choice of its style — that of an Edward I Castle. The architect, County Surveyor William Parsons, knew about scale and the historical associations of style but not about the effect of materials. As a result, the smoothly cut stone of the great gateway conveys the unfortunate impression that the building is an elaborate model built for a spectacular fantasy film. BELOW: William Flint designed the impressively plain Greek revival New Hall for the numerous but uninfluential Liberals in 1831. After functioning as the Mechanics Institute, it became the Free Library, a function it still serves.

ABOVE: Horsefair Street looking towards Gallowtree Gate: nothing now remains – on the right, is an entrance to the cattle market and the Three Crowns whose owner, William Bishop is remembered in nearby Bishop Street. BELOW: 'The Firs' on London Road is one of the earliest surviving houses in Stoneygate, now the Islamic Foundation.

Victorian Growth

The nineteenth century saw the transformation of Leicester from a small market town to one of the important urban centres of the country. It is not easy to trace its physical growth, since building, particularly in the case of houses, was piecemeal. As a result, a street laid out in one decade could still have a number of undeveloped plots decades later. For instance, Knighton Church Road was laid out by Isaac Barradale in 1874 but was not completely built up until the middle years of this century.

In addition to Southfields there were four growth areas which were close to the old town centre: the northern sections of the old medieval town, the area around St Margaret's, a wedge to the south-west and, biggest of all, the Wharf Street development.

After the sack of 1173, much of the area north of High Street remained undeveloped. The 1828 map shows that the large section west of Churchgate and south of Sanvey Gate only comprised Highcross Street, Cumberland Street, St John's Lane, St Peter's Lane, Elbow Lane and Freeschool Lane. But within eighteen years the following streets were added: Burgess Street, Durham Street, Grape Street, Junior Street, Long Lane, Olive Street, Vauxhall Street and White Street. The area now occupied by the St Margaret's' Bus Station also saw the rapid growth of tiny streets: Gravel Street, New Road, Osborne Street and Sandacre Street. Demolition has, of course, removed the houses and many of the streets.

In the 1830s and '40s, new streets were laid out around St Margaret's. These included Canning Place, Canning Street, Craven Street, Devonshire Street, Friday Street, Hull Street, Luke Street, Old Mill Lane and Pares Street. The boggy condition of land near the river forced the development in a north-easterly direction, where it eventually joined up with the growth around Navigation Street.

The wedge to the south-west has largely disappeared, but at one time the area between the canal and Aylestone Road was crowded with streets, houses and factories. Many of the long-gone streets south of Mill Lane must have pre-dated the middle of the century for, by the 1850s, infilling was taking palce. For instance, Laxton Street was laid in 1851 by William Henry Laxton and, further south, Aylestone Street was laid out in 1852. One or two of the later streets have survived, and there are some factories dating from the nineteenth century. St Andrew's, Jarrom Street also survives, but it looks lost amid the Polytechnic car parks.

Between the 1820s and the '70s a big wedge of housing grew up from south of Belgrave Gate to as far south as Humberstone Road, and as far east as Cobden Street – the Wharf Street development. Wharf Street itself, and some of the streets running off it such as Wheat Street, Carley Street and Brook Street, appear on the 1828 map, as also do Bedford Street (then called Barkby Lane), and a group of streets of Belgrave Gate: Britannia Street, Crabb Street, George Street, Grosvenor Street and Woodoy Street. And then in the 1830s and '40s Bow Street, Byron Street, Dryden Stret, Fennell Street, Fleet Street, Lee Street and Pike

Street were built off Bedford Street, and in the 1850s Crafton Street, Clyde Street, Erskine Street, Gladstone Street and Russell Square were laid out in the Wharf Street vicinity. Further east there was building in Brunswick Street, Curzon Street, and Stanley Street in the 1840s, and in Bright Street and Cobden Street a decade later. Taylor Street, at the north end of Curzon Street, was laid out by John Kelham in 1860. Building, particularly in the most northerly group of streets – Birstall Street, Syston Street and Willow Street – was still going on in the early years of the 1870s.

Few areas in Leicester have attracted as much loyal nostalgia as Wharf Street. If stories are true, the people were clannish, tough, cheerful and independent. Local heroes were butchers who catered for low incomes, or criminals who dodged the police. In some streets (specifically those between Bedford Street and Wharf Street) there were dozens of brothels, lodging houses, pubs, tiny lock-up shops and squalid little courts, where several families shared a single tap in a communal yard. Children attended the Ragged School in Bedford Street, Pike Street Board School, or the Wesleyan school in Clyde Street. There was a pinched-looking church by William Parsons – Christ Church, Bow Street (1838) – and a grand, spacious 'working man's Cathedral': the stone-faced St Matthew's by Scott, which now stands shut and neglected in the hard-edged wilderness of the St Matthew's Estate. Indeed, only a tiny fragment of this myth-ridden area (the 'Elephant Man' was born in Lee Street in 1862, and the brides-in-the-bath murderer contracted his only legal marriage while living in Wharf Street) survives, and that looks tame and lost: a few houses on Wharf Street, the one time Empire on the corner of Gladstone Street, the gaunt Zion Chapel on Erskine Street and, hidden away in the Estate, the four-square Curzon Street Chapel, built in 1859 by Flint and Shenton.

All the other areas are outside the medieval core. To the north-east there is Belgrave Road; to the east and south-east Highfields, Spinney Hill and North Evington; to the south Stoneygate, Clarendon Park, Knighton Fields and Aylestone Park; to the west beyond the river West End, Narborough Road, Tudor Road and Newfoundpool; and finally, to the north, the area around Woodgate.

The Belgrave Road area was developed from the 1870s. James Bird laid out Cranbourne Street, Gresham Street and, to the south, Catherine Street in 1870. In 1873 he added Argyle Street and Dorset Street. Off Catherine Street he laid out Belper Street and Martin Street in 1875. Most of the streets on the northern side of Belgrave Road were built in the 1880s and '90s. Architect Arthur Hardy was building in Garfield Street in 1882, and James Hunt in Olphin Street in 1885. In the 1890s there was building in Bruin, Cooper, Coral and Wand Streets. South of Belgrave Road, Rendell Street, which overlooks the Cossington Street recreation ground, was also developed in the 1890s. The only exception to the later pattern of houses furthest away from the centre is the development near road junctions – Melton Turn and the point where Marfitt Street crosses Melton Road to become Checketts Road. In Halkin Street, near Melton Turn, there is a house with gothic detailing dated 1879, and beyond Checketts Road there is a house dated 1877. Development continued into this century, Dundonald Road, Hunter Road and Macdonald Road still being built up in 1902. The St Mark's Estate has replaced some of the earlier roads, but most of the development survives.

To the east there was expansion along Humberstone Road. Morledge Street and Midland Street were laid out in the mid 1840s, there was building in William Street in the 1850s, and in Ann Street and Richard Street in the 1860s. Also in the '60s there was building, further east, in Sussex Street and Walter Street. Further out, beyond the railway bridge, Forest Road, Ash Street, Oak Street, Elm Street, Larch Street and Beech Street were built up in the late 1860s and early '70s, while in the 1880s and '90s this area spread further east, with the addition of Frisby and Willow Brook Roads. Demolition has transformed much of that (the new estate is thoughtful and attractive), as it has also done further east, where the suburb of West Humberstone is now a mere fragment.

The biggest development to the east was a large area of housing – Highfields, Spinney Hill, St Saviour's and North Evington – which stretches from south of Humberstone Road to London Road, Evington Road and East Park Road. Building took over fifty years and, what is more important, it occurred in a number of local centres, which gradually joined up. Nowadays it seems homogeneous; this is because it is done in Leicester brick and much of it is terraced, a building type which, for all the variety it makes possible, imposes uniformity.

Building began in the 1840s in two places: Kent Street off Humberstone Road and, near London Road, Conduit Street and Sparkenhoe Street. Beal Street was built off Kent Street in 1860, and in 1861 people were living in Garendon Street, Berners Street and Upper Kent Street. Off Sparkenhoe Street, Lincoln Street was laid out by James Frank Smith in 1860, and another architect and surveyor, A.C. Macaulay, added Hobart Street and Seymour Street in 1863. These two areas were joined when Upper Kent Street met Upper Conduit Street.

The major period of expansion was the 1870s – not surprisingly, given the huge growth in population in the previous decade. There was building in Melbourne Street, Maynard Road and Charnwood Street, and a number of new roads: Turner Street in 1870, and Mafield and Murfield Streets in 1873 – all by James Bird. Further to the east, between Humberstone Road and Charnwood Street, there was building in Edward Street, Farnham Street, Flint Street, Mount Street, Shenton Street and Sherrard Street. New streets included the nearby Frederick Street and Wood Hill, both of which were laid out in 1877. There was considerable expansion near London Road: Sax Coburg Street dates from 1869. As Tichborne Street was extended to the south, a number of roads were built off it. James Bird laid out St Stephen's Road and Bartholomew Street in 1874 and Biddulph Street in 1875. Joseph Goddard laid out Welland and Avon Street in 1876, Medway Street in 1877 and, off Biddulph Street Chandos and Sutherland Streets in 1876 and Lonsdale and Roslyn Streets in 1877. New streets were laid out east of Sparkenhoe Street: some, like Earl Howe Street and Twycross Street (1877) ran to the south, while Gopsall Street (1873) ran to the east. All these were the work of A.C. Macaulay, who was also responsible for Oxendon Street in 1873 and for the extension of Clipstone Street in 1877. In 1879 he further joined the two areas of Kent Street and Sparkenhoe Street when he extended Melbourne Road from Clipstone Street to St Peter's Road.

That link made possible building to the south, near the old boundary of Mere Road. It looks as if, during the 1880s, streets were built up from both the Melbourne Road and Mere Road ends. There was a lot of building in Diseworth, Donnington and Worthington Streets between 1882 and 1884. Also in 1882, H.R. Harding laid out Skipworth Street, Onslow Street and Guilford Street. The wedge between Tichborne Street and Evington Street was filled in by Arthur Wakerley in 1886, when he drew up plans for St Alban's Road, Churchill Street, Connaught Street and Hamilton Street.

North Evington was developed in the 1890s. The idea for this little industrial village south of Mere Road came from Arthur Wakerley. He planned a village-style community of terraced houses, factories, shops, a post office and, round the little market square, a fire station, police station and town hall. The architecture is loud, the scale is small. Wakerley was fond of mixing Flemish, Elizabethan and neo-Baroque details, so the result is a rather fussy, though decidedly jolly miniature monumentality. At the top of the hill there broods the domed Wesley Hall and the great tower of the Imperial Hotel – once, for Wakerley was a Methodist and a teetotaller, without a licence for beers and spirits. Off the precipitous Granby Avenue (too steep for horses) he built Prospect Hill, Halstead Street with its little flight of steps into

Wood Hill (Leicester feels more like Bradford or Blackburn at this point), Asfordby Street, Baggrave Street and Rolleston Street. He did not, however, design all the buildings – some are much too plain for that. At the moment the area is undergoing an exciting re-furbishment scheme prepared by the Rod Hackney partnership.

Beyond North Evington there was a great deal of building in the 1890s. East of Green Lane Road there are the 'hunting streets' – Quorn, Fernie and Meynell – and south of East Park Road there was building throughout the decade in places such as Dorothy Road, Moat Road, Osborne Road, Orson Street and Stanhope Street.

It is difficult to know what to make of this big area of housing. There is collective guilt about Highfields and, by association, the areas beyond. It was so clearly a good place to live (look at the big terraces on Highfields Street and Tichborne Street), and yet quite early in the twentieth century it fell into multi-occupation, and there followed the symptoms of what is now called inner city decay – dereliction, vice and, among non-residents, a reluctance to visit it. Hence, perhaps, the City Council's thoughful rehabilitation schemes: new lamp-posts, new garden walls with attractive railings, the cleaning of brickwork, tree planting and the blocking off of roads. It has worked. There is now more pride and more interest. And there are things to be proud of and interested in: a variety of architectural styles, the amazing architecture of Melbourne Hall (Goddard, 1881), some good street corners, lots of useful shops and, to the south, Spinney Hill Park. The whole area is best seen on a sunny autumn day, when the rusty leaves in the Park tone in with the deep red of Leicester brick, and when the soft shadows cast by the weakening sun pick out brick cornices, moulded door heads and the patterned stone-work above the windows.

To the south east of Leicester is Stoneygate – one of Leicester's longest established suburbs. We think of it (rightly) as a fine Victorian development, but often forget that, with the sale of big gardens, it is one which is still growing. Its history goes back to the early decades of the nineteenth century, when it was still part of Blaby. The Firs on London Road must be 1820s, and the big house which is now in Springfield Road could be 1840s. But the main periods of expansion were the 1870s, '80s and '90s. (Was it popular because, among other things, rates were cheaper than in Leicester?) Unlike Highields, we are not dealing with a great volume of building; there are not many houses, but most of them are quite large and stand in generous grounds overlooking broad and now leafy roads. It is Leicester's most sophisticated suburb: a spacious upper middle-class development of thoughtfully designed houses. Stoneygate (the name is used broadly, as is the Leicester custom) grew in three places: the Knighton Church Road, Holbrook Road and Sidney Road area; the Ratcliffe Road, Elms Road and Knighton Drive area; and, nearer the town, the area around Stoneygate Road.

Shenton and Baker laid out Sidney Road in 1876, and there was building in Knighton Church Road from 1877 onwards. There was also building, albeit only two or three houses at a time, throughout the later decades in Goldhill Road, Holbrook Road and South Knighton Road. Much of the earliest work of Frank Seale, who was later to establish himself as a prominent domestic architect, was done in Holbrook Road.

The houses in the second area were much more substantial: among the earliest are Stockdale Harrison's appropriately gothic almshouses, which were built in 1876 in Knighton Drive. In 1880 R.J. Goodacre built an English vernacular house for Harry Gee at the corner of London Road and Knighton Road, and also in that year Edward Burgess built a big Elizabethan house – Knighton Hayes in Ratcliffe Road. Four years later Joseph Goddard designed the sumptuous yet straggling Knighton Spinneys for himself: it is bold English vernacular – hanging tile and lovely oriel windows – and has a red lodge that juts out from the building line so as to be visible from both ends of the curving road. Perhaps not to be outdone, Ellis, the owner of Knighton Hayes, commissioned Burgess a year later to build a lodge – and he went one better by having it built on the corner of London Road!

Off Stoneygate Road, James Frank Smith laid out Alexandra Road in 1876, and Millican added Albert Road in 1878. Issaac Barradale laid out Springfield Road and Cross Road in 1884, and in 1887 added St John's Road, which contains two of his own houses. Most of the houses in these streets are substantial, so it is something of a surprise to come across two streets of terraced buildings – Francis Street and Allandale Road. In the 1870s James Frank Smith drew up a plan for the Stoneygate area that contained no terraced housing, but the plots failed to attract buyers, so by the 1880s he was building terraced houses in Francis Street. Later, in 1890, Goddard drew up a plan to give some coherence to the area. Calling it the Stoneygate Road Estate, he planned more small buildings in Allandale Road to complement Francis Street, and larger houses with black and white timbering in the gables in Stoughton Road.

Contemporary with Francis Street was another area of terraced housing – Clarendon Park. The Clarendon Park Estate Company was established in 1877 to develop land previously owned by the Craddock family of Knighton Hall. Shenton and Baker were surveyors, though most of the houses were done by builders such as Ellingworth, Harris Holland and Orton. It grew in two directions: spreading west from the junction of Queens Road and Clarendon Park Road and, on a smaller scale, spreading east from Welford Road. In 1879 Queen's Road was extended to join Victoria Park Road, and Montague Road was laid out. Cecil (now Cecilia) Road and part of Howard Road followed in 1881, and in 1882 St Leonard's Road, Edward Road, Oxford Road, Craddock Road and Seymour Road were added. Near Welford Road, there was building in Fleetwood Road and Leopold Road from 1879 onwards. Gradually the two areas joined. Bulwer Road and Lytton Road were added in 1892, Hartopp and Adderley in 1894, and in 1895 Lorne Road was extended northwards towards Victoria Park Road. The map of 1903 shows that the western end of Howard Road and the northern ends of Hartopp, Lytton and Lorne Roads were yet to be built up. By 1915 building was complete, and by 1930 houses were appearing further to the south in Greenhill, Landseer, Burlington, Raeburn and Gainsborough Roads. Recently, the intimate little streets of Clarendon Park have acquired a new character: the blocking off of roads, planting of trees and estabishing of play areas have gone hand in hand with the arrival of 'progressive' residents.

Further south and to the west of Welford Road another development took place round Knighton Fields. The railway has a powerful effect on the area: visually it provides the drama of the great blue arches on Knighton Lane, and it splits the development into a group of streets off Knighton Lane East – Wordsworth Road, Kingsley Road, Cowper Street, Burns and Scott Streets – and a smaller group off Knighton Lane West – Shakespeare Street, Sheridan Street, Thackeray Street and Macaulay Street. Frank Seale acted as surveyor and architect for many of the terraced houses. In 1890 he laid out Knighton Fields East, Wordsworth Road, Cowper Street, Byron Street, Kingsley Street, and all the above mentioned streets off Knighton Fields West.

Knighton Fields is close to the charming and rather isolated Aylestone Park – a little network of streets, some short and some curving, built on slightly hilly ground between Aylestone Road and Saffron Lane. Building went on from the 1870s. For instance, Milligan Road and Duncan Road were laid out in 1877 by James Bird. As a Victorian suburb it is almost complete: there is a good corner where Richmond Road and Lansdowne Road meet, given scale by a library and a simple brick church of 1891 by R.J. Goodacre, and by a large house dated 1873. Elsewhere there are little shops, small factories and, on the junction of Cavendish Road and Richmond Road, a rather good Italianate Methodist Chapel of 1883.

Development west of Leicester was held up by the persistence of big estates, notably Danett's Hall and Westcotes. Nearer the river, however, there was the 'West End' – streets of terraced houses built up from the 1850s. Flint and Shenton laid out Leamington Street, Thorpe Street and New Park Street on vacant land between Hinckley Road and what we now know as King Richard's Road. There was building in the 1860s, but it was the 1870s that saw rapid expansion, with much work done in Arundel Street, Buckingham Street, Catesby Street, Fitzroy Street and Norfolk Street. In 1878 the houses expanded beyond the Fosse Road when the Borough surveyor, F.L. Stephens, laid out the eastern stretch of Glenfield Road and all the streets adjoining it as far as Neville Road. The visual centre of West End was the enormous Emmanuel Baptist Church (Shenton and Baker 1871), which for years dominated the little terraces and, converted to warehouses, survived the demolition of the area till a fire destroyed it. Its great octagonal drum rising above the chimney pots spoke of the power of non-conformity in a town often called the capital of dissent.

Three other areas west of the river were later developments. The demolition of Westcotes led to building off Hinckley and Narborough Roads. Cranmer Street, Ridley Street, Latimer Street, Tyndale Street, Shaftesbury Street, Luther Street and Livingstone Street, collectively known as the 'Martyr' Roads, were laid out in 1885 by William Millican. Much of the early building was done by Redfern and Sawday. There was building on Narborough Road throughout the 1890s, and also in that decade there was industrial growth along Western Road.

The Tudor Road area was contemporary with expansion on Narborough Road. In 1895 Goddard and Paget extended the already existing Tudor Road and added Warren Street, Paget Street, Vaughan Street, Tewkesbury Street, Danett Street, Tyrell Street and, the boundary of the development, a section of Fosse Road. Mantle Road Board School was built in 1896 (Edwad Burgess), and a big factory by a Northampton architect, Charles Dorman, was built on Tudor Road in 1900. Also in that year Goddard built a good arts and crafts pub on the corner of Tewkesbury Road and Tudor Road. But after that, Tudor Road seems to have been forgotten. It had a cinema – The Tudor – which closed; the comforts of religion were withdrawn shortly after the First World War when a mission church, St Silas's, Warren Street, was closed, and more recently the school was shut. The effect of streamlining King Richard's Road, it must be said, has further isolated it. (When, some years ago, I led a walk there, many in the group said they didn't even know it existed.)

The other western development was Newfoundpool. In the 1890s ten streets were laid out between Beatrice Road and Pool Road. When built, they formed a wedge projecting into the countryside just south of the Glenfield railway. A barn of a church was provided in 1899 (R.J. Goodacre), a Board School in Ingle Street and, at the turn of the century, a Methodist Chapel was re-erected on Fosse Road, having been moved from St Nicholas Street to make way for the Central Railway.

Development to the north can be dealt with quickly. The river prevented a great deal of growth, though off Woodgate William Millican laid out the vanished Bradgate Street, Crystal Street, Diamond Street, Littleton Street and Opal Street in 1872, and in the 1890s there was the small development of Bassett Street, Dunton Street and Marshall Street.

OPPOSITE ABOVE: One of an exciting series of photographs taken in the late 1860s or early 1870s from the steeple of St Martin's, looking north east. In the bottom right hand corner Carts Lane runs north to meet the High Street. To the right in High Street is the tower of Lord's Place (town house of the Earls of Huntingdon). On the far left is Salem Chapel in Freeschool Lane and to the top left St Margaret's Church. In the centre is the Fielding Johnson works, and to its left the Great Meeting Chapel, school and the wooden warehouse on Churchgate.

BELOW: This 1861 photograph, taken from Humberstone Gate, shows the Old Haymarket which, having served as assembly rooms and shops, was replaced by the Clock Tower.

ABOVE: Granby street retains much that is nineteenth century. Its two biggest losses are the Britannia Works and the Temperance Hall. LEFT: Behind the graveyard of Great Meeting stands this warehouse built c1830 by a carpenter called Lawrence Brown and later used by his son, Thomas Daniel Brown, as the head office of a building firm. It was in use till the mid-1970s, when the Council saved it from demolition. RIGHT: Virtually nothing now remains of old Belgrave Gate. The houses to the right were demolished when the Haymarket was built, and the big factory on the left was pulled down in the late 1970s. It was built in 1870 by William Jackson as a boot and shoe factory for Stead and Simpson.

ABOVE: Top Hat Terrace on London Road was designed (1864) by James Frank Smith, son of policeman 'Tanky' Smith, who had been hired by the Winstanleys of Braunstone to look for Squire Winstanley, missing on a European tour. 'Tanky' traced him to Koblenz, where his body was found in a lake. Handsomely paid, he invested the money in land, building this terrace in honour of himself (the carved heads represent him in a number of disguises) and developing Francis Street in Stoneygate. Note the now vanished front gardens, one of which survived into the 1960s. BELOW: Houses on Navigation Street with a gas holder in the distance. The first Gas Works were built by the Canal in 1821.

ABOVE: A corner pawnbroker's shop on Mill Lane; right – Court A led to a little terrace built in the yard behind. LEFT: Rathbone Place, a short thoroughfare off East Street, mentioned in directories as early as 1846, is typical of streets of little 'cottages' that, until the 1950s, could be found near the City centre. RIGHT: Bateman's yard, off Sandacre Street, must have been built in the 1820s or 1830s and was demolished in the 1930s, when the St Margaret's Bus Station was built.

LEFT: The area around Wharf Street was once full of doss houses. This building on the corner of Britannia Street and Belgrave Road was the last, still in use in the late 1960s. RIGHT: A fragment of old Wharf Street: left, two shops designed by Isaac Barradale in 1880, and right, Leicester's only surviving Victorian Theatre – the Hippodrome (later the Empire) built in 1892 by W. Hancock. BELOW: The junction of Belgrave Gate and Bedford Street was much more important in the nineteenth century: BelgraveGate was the road north, and Bedford Street led into the highly populated Wharf Street area.

LEFT: On the corner of Highfields and Tichborne Streets is Arthur Wakerley's Synagogue (1898); Wakerley, a staunch Methodist, produced a design which is convincingly religious without being obviously Christian. RIGHT: James Bird was one of the most prolific architects of Victorian Leicester, but because most of his work consisted of terraced houses (or cottages as they were called) little of it survives. This terrace in Tichborne Street of 1876 did. BELOW: Knighton Drive: the house to the left is Miss Barlow's Almshouses of 1876 by Stockdale Harrison. Beyond are houses T. P. Bown built as a complete terrace in 1898.

ABOVE: Knighton Drive: the first two houses are by T.P. Born (1886, 1899), while the third and fourth are by Goddard (1891) and Millican (1879). BELOW: Allandale Road was largely built up by Goddard in the early 1890s as part of his plan for the Stoneygate Road Estate. It joined the already existing Francis Street, much of which was built by James Frank Smith.

LEFT: This shed and public lavatory on the boundary of Leicester and Oadby was originally a tram shed, and for some years, an industrial museum. RIGHT: Ashfordby Street is the main thoroughfare of North Evington: on the corner is the Anchor works, later a co-operative to build Humberstone Garden suburb; next, the Fire Station (1899) and beyond, the Police Station. BELOW: Leicester west of the river developed later than other parts of the town because of two big estates: Westcotes (demolished in 1885) and Danett's Hall, the latter near the present King Richard's Road, off (foreground) Watts Causeway. In 1859 its owner, Dr Noble, held a garden party for 1200 to celebrate John Bigg's election victory. Two years later he died, and the house was demolished to make way for terraced housing.

ABOVE: North Evington 'Town Hall' as seen from Wood Hill: Wakerley built it in 1890 and it is now the Conservative Club, and thus the only Town Hall in the City where Tories have power. LEFT: Granby Avenue, North Evington, is the closest safe, villagey Leicester ever comes to the drama of the industrial north. The Avenue was laid out by Arthur Wakerley when he planned his little industrial community. RIGHT: When the London Road station was built in 1892 a large 1860 Methodist Chapel was demolished. Arthur Wakerley, a Methodist, rescued the pediment and the four columns and re-erected them on the front of a factory in Rolleston Street. They were finally demolished in 1960.

A temple to travel.
ABOVE: Leicester's first and grandest station was built in Campbell Street in 1840. For years it was thought to be the work of William Flint, but recent research has shown it to come from William Parsons.

LEFT: Given the impact organised holidays have had on our century, Thomas Cook was one of the most influential men of our modern world. He was brought up in Belgrave, organised his first trip to Loughborough, attended Archdeacon Lane Chapel, lived on London Road and is buried in Welford Road Cemetery. RIGHT: Isaac Barradale's office in Greyfriars, designed in 1876 and built in 1880, was one of the first buildings in Leicester to introduce the then highly fashionable English Vernacular style. And between 1881 and 1885 Ernest Gimson worked here when he was articled to Barradale.

Men of Property

What were those Victorian houses like? The vast majority were small, brick, and built in terraces, though building was done in small groups, often of no more than five or six at a time. If one takes a walk along a street of terraced houses one can see the changes in detailing around the doors, windows and beneath the eaves. These terraced houses were usually called 'cottages' by their builders and architects. Except in rare cases such as Mill Hill Lane where they have little front gardens, the cottages opened directly onto the street from a door in the front room or, in the case of larger ones, a narrow hall. In most cases there were three rooms downstairs and three upstairs. The privy was in the garden. One variation was the placing of the door. For instance, in Bartholomew Street, the doors are situated off long passages, leading from the pavement.

Who built them? Most were builders such as Gilbert and Pipes, H.T. Mortimer and Rolleston and Stimpson, although others such as George Brown and W.S. Burton later styled themselves architects, and some were architects who either worked for small developers as well as wealthier clients or started on terraced housing before finding bigger commissions. Joseph Goddard is an example of the former, and Frank Seale of the latter.

None of the firms were large (few survived into the twentieth century), but between them they built thousands of houses for a rapidly expanding population. Predictably, they tended to work in a limited number of localities. Harry Orton, for instance, built 117 houses between 1880 and 1887, all of them in Clarendon Park. A much bigger firm of architects, Redfern and Sawday, built 260 houses between 1876 and 1880, but they were mostly in the Highfields or Westcotes areas. They were not the most prolific. H.R. Harding on his own and in partnership with W.T. Toppott built over 500 houses between 1876 and 1885. James Bird and W.S. Burton also had, by Leicester standards, a big output. Bird built over 400 houses in the Belgrave, Wharf Street, Highfields and Clarendon Park areas between 1870 and 1880. Burton on his own and, from 1873, in partnership with Willoughby, built over four hundred houses between 1870 and 1879 in West End, Humberstone Road, Wharf Street, St Saviour's, Highfields and Clarendon Park and, like Bird, much of what he built has been demolished.

Money, of course, is evident behind all the building that went on. It was, however, more evident in the houses of the comfortable middle and upper-middle classes. Money could buy ample space – those big Stoneygate gardens – and also style. Whereas the terraced house, apart from one or two with gothic decoration (there are some in Francis Street), was essentially (and attractively) styleless, the larger villas (the most common name for them) were Italianate, though it must be admitted in a stripped form. Saxby Street, with work by Burton and Willoughby, James Frank Smith and William Millican, is the best example in Leicester. But after the 1880s those who could afford style went neither for Italian nor definitely for Gothic: they were attracted to English revival styles – Elizabethan, whether in brick with gables or with black and white timber work; vernacular with hanging tiles and coving; Queen Anne with tall sash windows punched into an embellished brick facade or, in a few rare cases, Arts and Crafts with big Swithland slate roofs, overhanging eaves and metal brackets supporting the guttering. The architects who worked in these styles were again local: Isaac Barradale, T.P. Bown, Edward Burgess, T.H. Fosbrooke, R.J. Goodacre, Goddard and Paget, Stockdale Harrison, William Millican, Redfern and Sawday and James Tait.

Isaac Barradale was the first to build in the then new English Revival style. His own office in Greyfriars, designed in 1876 and built in 1880, is still one of Leicester's most remarkable buildings, with a confident first floor window stretching almost the entire length of the facade. In Stoneygate he built large semi-detached houses in Knighton Drive, Stoneygate Road, Alexandra Road, Knighton Road, Knighton Park Road and Clarendon Park Road. If there is a 'Leicester style' – tall gables, roughcast, heavy timbering, small-paned windows – Isaac Barradale is its most characteristic exponent. Goddard and Paget introduced timber work at Brookfield in 1877 and in 1879 built an important pair of semis on the corner of Princess Road and West Walk; as a composition they are a mess, but their details – hanging tile, coving and the fashionable sunflower motif – mark another important stage in the introduction of English Vernacular features. Their best work came later – the artsy crafty Ratcliffe Lodge of 1896 and, in Stoneygate Road, the aptly named Red House of 1900. Stockdate Harrison lived into the twentieth century and with his talented son Shirley (architect of the De Montfort Hall and the Usher Hall in Edinburgh) built some lovely Arts and Crafts houses: St Michael's Belgrave Vicarage, 1897, All Souls Vicarage 1910 and Shirley's own house, Four Gables in Elms Road, also of 1910. Most famous of all was Ernest Gimson who had been articled to Barradale. His two houses – Inglewood of 1892 and The White House of 1897 –are masterpieces: Inglewood, in Elizabeth Williamson's apt phrase, is 'rural sweetness and light', and The White House has perhaps the two loveliest domestic interiors in Leicester – the dining room with broad split oak panelling and, adjoining it, a warm and civilized lounge overlooking the garden.

For the man in the street (even in Leicester where they are dedicated savers) money means shopping. One transformation wrought by the Victorians was that of turning Leicester into a shopping centre. Of course, there were shops before, but there were no terraced corner shops or big, purpose-built town centre stores. In Leicester a satisfying number survive.

The terraced corner shop was purpose-built. At one time there were more than there are now, but during the 1930s a number closed, never to be re-opened. These can usually be identified, as the wooden pilasters and large windows remain. A number of building plans survive showing say, six cottages and one shop. Some streets had many shops. The legendary – and therefore demolished – Charnwood Street bustled with communal life until the late 1960s. The best surviving local shops can now be found off the Belgrave Road and in North Evington. A slightly more up-market development is a large gabled and timbered terrace of shops built in 1897 by George Brown on the corner of Braunstone Gate and Hinckley Road. It remains a busy frontage – both commerically and architecturally.

In the town centre there are a number of buildings which are meant to catch the eye. Leicester is a modest place, yet it allowed flourishes when it came to shopping. Goodacre used a kind of fourteenth century Gothic for Hollingworth's wine vaults, built in 1868 on the corner of Horsefair Street, overlooking Pocklington's Walk. Even more imperious is Isaac Barradale's Germanic corner gable on Joseph Johnson's (now Fenwick's), which commands attention from Market Street, Belvoir Street, King Street and Welford Place. In Market Street is Millican and Smith's allegorical fantasy – the Midland Auction Mart of 1876. At the centre of a much carved facade is a bust of Mercury, the point of which, no doubt, is that transactions are speedy and you, the purchaser, are a god in the commercial realm. More sober, and appropriately so, was the short-lived Funeral Warehouse built in 1870 in the Market Place by William Millican. (It was, for many years, Broughton and Jones.) Many of these shops are still Victorian above the first floor but have lost their ground floor frontages. An exception is Pearce's in the Market Place, and the almost complete and deliciously Italianate Green's on Humberstone Gate, built in 1863 by James Frank Smith.

Green's functioned as a shop and as a brewery. Two aspects of that are important to an understanding of Leicester: the relation between making and selling, and the small-scale nature of the industry. The former factor produced small buildings which have since been converted into shops. On Granby Street there was a boot factory and shop, built in 1873 by Shenton and Baker, which later lost its manufacturing but not its retailing function. The second factor is also visually important. Leicester has no vast industrial complexes of the Victorian period. British Shoe on Belgrave Road and the St Margaret's works were not large till this century. The largest Victorian factory was Josiah Gimson's Vulcan Road Works, built in 1876 by J.B. Everard. It is a long, fairly severe building with, by comparison, a quite jolly Italian clock tower. It was not, as it is now, just a factory. In 1878 twenty-six workers' cottages and a mess room were built. A year later Everard added a warehouse and a bakehouse. It was then not unlike the big industrial complexes in the north, but it was small and did not survive as such.

Of the other Victorian factories none were large but many were attractive. Most were built for the hosiery, shoe or light engineering industries. Dick's shoe factory of 1875 on the corner of Colton and Rutland Streets is a grand, well-proportioned building in a subdued renaissance style. Much more striking – but also renaissance – is Faire's factory of 1895 in Rutland Street. There are few better in England, and it was the work of a local man – Edward Burgess. Nowhere in this clean, small-scale City do factories crowd out the skyline. Occasionally, on bleak November evenings, a glance along York Street can convince the passer-by that he or she really is in Manchester, and the view along Wheat Street, dominated as it is by James Bird's plain 1870 factory, is distinctively northern. But such views are not typical. Most Leicester factories are small, finely detailed with large windows divided off by brick pilasters. There are good ones on Millstone Lane and Stamford Street, and how many cities can boast, as we can, of a Queen Anne factory – Downings of 1881 – on the corner of Newarke Stret and Pocklington's Walk? It was built by James Tait. Leicester's warehouses are also friendly. Barrow Brothers on the corner of Albion and Belvoir Street is by Tait, and Queen Street is by Harding and Toppott. This 1897 building is a shade more lavish, with much brick moulding and a rudimentary tower.

Money is evident in so many buildings. Of the gentleman's clubs the most grandly sited was Goddard's Leicestershire Club of 1875. From its great bowed front there are good views down Welford Road to the Gaol. The pubs were not as large and opulent as those in Nottingham (Leicester people have always thought of Nottingham as sinful), but one of them, Millican's the Pelican of 1881 in Gallowtree Gate, had both a racy reputation and, until recently, a lovely frontage of plaster, brick and tasteful wooden balconies. And there were theatres: the great Theatre Royal by Parsons of 1836 (now demolished), Phipps's Royal. Opera House in Silver Street of 1876, (demolished and replaced by the Malcolm Arcade) and, most wonderful of all, an oriental dream of an interior provided by Frank Matcham, the most celebrated of all theatre designers, in 1900 for the Palace Theatre on Belgrave Gate (yes: demolished). Now only the white-washed Empire, built by W. Hancock of London in 1892, survives on Wharf Street.

Two kinds of building remain: offices and banks. Though more sober than theatres, they nevertheless provided some grand architecture. The purpose-built office was a Victorian invention. Flint built the Phoenix Building in 1842, but most came later. Kirby and Bromley, a Nottingham firm, built a gothic office for a solicitor's firm in Market Street in 1879, and five years later Goodacre put up a rather French-looking block on the corner of Halford Street and Gallowtree Gate. One of the nicest is Arthur Wakerley's Tudor building of 1887 for Whetstone and Frost's in Bishop Street, and the grandest work came from Goddard and Paget, who did the Sun Alliance of 1891 in Horsefair Street and the renaissance headquarters for Thomas Cook, built in 1894 in Gallowtree Gate. The little panels of four railway journeys remain, though the ground floor has been destroyed.

Banks had to be grand in order to advertise their wealth and reliability. Millican's National Provincial Bank (now National Westminster) of 1869 on the corner of Granby Street and Horsefair Street is less than fifty yards from Goddard's Leicestershire Bank (now Midland Bank) of 1870. Toegether they compete in a 'battle of the styles': Millican conservative and Italian, Goddard progressively Gothic and, with French and even Moorish features, eclectic; Millican used white brick, Goddard fierce red brick and terracotta; Millican used standard Italian mouldings, Goddard loosed Samuel Barfield on the building to spawn a brood of impish little monsters that cling to the surface and, to complete the opposition, outside architecture, Millican was a Tory and Goddard a Liberal. The two banks are not only advertisements for the services of the two institutions but a visual parable of the clash of styles in Victorian architecture.

Yet even grander is Everard and Pick's St Martin's Bank. Designed in 1899 for Pares, taken over by Parrs, it eventually became the property of the Westminster and then the National Westminster Bank. It is a glorious essay in 'land of hope and glory' Baroque: columns, rustication, classical friezes, cupolas and, inside, a dome. Not even Chatwin's Lloyd's Bank of 1903 (a Birmingham architect building a Birmingham bank) can match the swagger and confidence of Everard and Pick's masterpiece.

These banks talked rather than listened, and what they said was about the power of money. But other buildings had other things to say; as well as the architecture of money, there was also the architecture of belief.

One of the achievements of Victorian architecture was that much loved building – the semi-detached house. In Leicester Isaac Barradale built his chosen design in Clarendon Park Road, Knighton Road and here, on rising ground, on Stoneygate Road, (1887).

ABOVE: The re-building of Brookfield marks a crucial stage in the visual history of Leicester. The house originally belonged to the Burgess family, but in the 1870s they sold it to the Fielding-Johnsons, who rebuilt it. In 1876 the lodge was designed by Goddard and Paget, and a year later the whole front of the house was remodelled in the black and white English vernacular manner – the first house in Leicester to be given that treatment. In the 1920s, the Diocese of Leicester purchased it as the Bishop's Lodge. It is now the Charles Frears Nursing School. LEFT: This house, designed by R.J. Goodacre in 1877, stands on the corner of Regent and Granville Roads. It was built for Joseph Wallis Goddard, an architect, who founded Goddard's Silver Polish. RIGHT: This terrace of four three-storeyed houses stands on Regent Road; it was designed by Goddard and Paget in 1881.

LEFT: Draper and Walters were the architects of this 1893 building on Springfield Road. Later Walters went into Parliament and in the 1920s was active in a number of housing schemes for miners in Derbyshire, Nottinghamshire and Yorkshire. RIGHT: An interestng house built for an important man: Mr Morley, owner of a big department store on Cheapside, had this house built by his brother in 1870 on the corner of Princess Road and De Montfort Street. BELOW: These two substantial houses in the Elizabethan manner were built by Goddard and Paget on the corner of London and St John's Roads in 1889.

LEFT: These semi-detached houses on St John's Road may reflect the joint efforts of master architect Isaac Barradale and his assistant, Amos Hall in 1887. Hall took over Barradale's firm in 1892. RIGHT: Knighton Spinneys: this rambling, pleasing, but pretty incoherent facade looks like Joseph Goddard's attempt to employ every detail of the English Vernacular style in one building. CENTRE: The lodge for Knighton Hayes, on the corner of London Road and Ratcliffe Road (1885) by Edward Burgess. BELOW LEFT: The White House was built in 1897 by Ernest Gimson for his brother Arthur. RIGHT: 'Inglewood' – the house Ernest Gimson designed for himself in 1892 but never occupied. Gimson was considered by Sir Niklaus Pevsner to be Britain's most important artist craftsman.

ABOVE: Battle of the styles, part one: William Millican's National Provincial Bank of 1869 is conservative, sober and restrained. LEFT: Battle of the styles, part two: Joseph Goddard's Leicestershire Bank of 1872 is conspicuously youthful. RIGHT: Leicester's grandest bank: built for Pares by Everard and Pick in 1899, taken over by Parrs (the P monogram woven into the decoration was therefore still appropriate), it now functions as the National Westminster Bank.

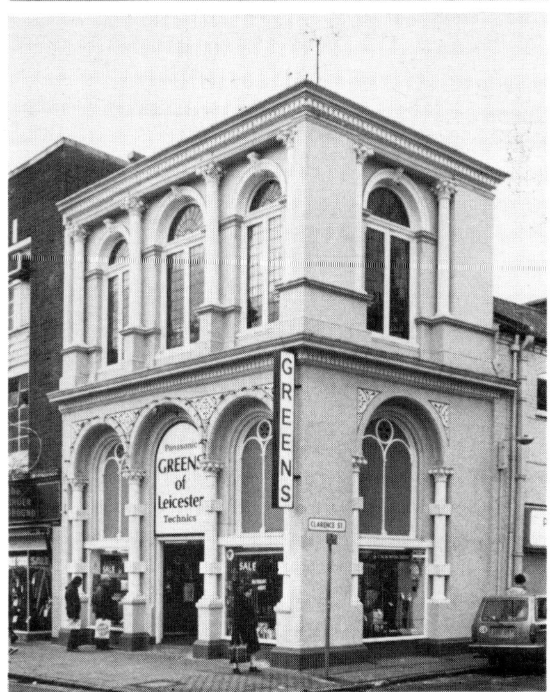

ABOVE LEFT: Chatwin of Birmingham built their bank for Lloyds in the High Street in 1903. RIGHT: The Victorian commercial gaiety of Market Street: Joseph Johnson's shop built in 1884 by Isaac Barradale, left, a turret which originally belonged to a hotel, also the work of Barradale. BELOW LEFT: The quite rapid development of Leicester in the 1870s and 1880s left a number of difficult plots. The junction of the lower section of New Walk and King Street was eventually developed in 1887 when Stockdale Harrison built three shops. RIGHT: Green's is one of the best of Leicester's Victorian shops. The Italian front of 1863 is the work of James Frank Smith.

ABOVE LEFT: This rather baronial turret of 1913 surmounts Stretton's factory on Castle Street, the work of Keites, Fosbrooke and Bedingfield. RIGHT: The Faire building on the corner of Rutland Street and Southampton Street is one of the finest late Victorian factories in England, designed by Edward Burgess in 1895. The fine dome is a feature, unfortunately lost. BELOW LEFT: Vulcan Works, built in 1876 by J.B. Everard for Josiah Gimson, was the largest industrial complex of Victorian Leicester. Here the huge beam engines for the Pumping Station (now the Museum of Technology) were cast. RIGHT: This 1888 factory in York Street is the work of Arthur Wakerley.

LEFT: A boot and shoe factory built by Shenton and Baker in 1873 for Bruin and Sons. Its position, in a busy section of Granby Street, makes it typical of the way small-scale Leicester industrial premises existed alongside houses and shops. ABOVE: William Flint designed this worsted spinning mill for J. Whitmore before 1844. BELOW: Shenton and Baker built a number of fine warehouses, many of which have been demolished. One survivor is this one on Lower Brown Street. It was designed in 1871 for Wale's, and its plain, functional frontage has remained unchanged.

ABOVE: A Queen Anne factory and a gentleman's club stand together on Welford Place. The factory, Downing's, was built in 1882 by James Tait, and the club, the Leicestershire, was designed in 1875 by Joseph Goddard. The statue is of John Biggs, hosier, Mayor and Liberal MP. Leicester's grandest Post Office was built on the corner of Granby and Bishop Streets in 1887. BELOW: The Leicestershire Bank is on the further side of Bishop Street, beyond which is a coffee house, later the Picture House.

A Battle of Buildings

Architecture can be the expression of moral views as well as of economic power. The nineteenth century town was the battleground not only of differing architectural styles but of competing social, political and religious interests. Leicester's buildings express, even preach, the beliefs and aspirations of those who built them. There is a clear visual tension between the religious establishment (and that of Leicester was both church and chapel) and the growing power of civic or simply secular interests. They, like the churches and the chapels, competed for the allegiance of the people by seeking to provide for what they saw as their deepest needs. This tension is not always a dramatic one, but the question of belief and values is nonetheless one of the strongest pressures behind many of the most impressive buildings of Victorian Leicester.

Think of a few Leicester scenes: the glimpses of the Cathedral steeple from Guildhall Lane, New Street or Silver Street; the proud front of the registrar's office (originally the poor law offices built in 1883 by Redfern and Sawday) on Pocklington's Walk; the great frontage of the YMCA at the end of Granby Street; the dominating presence of Charnwood Street School when approached from Nedham Street; the solidly massed dome of Wesley Hall and the steeple of St Saviour's Church and, adjoining them, the ample spaces of Spinney Hill Park. In different ways they are all claims to moral authority and power.

This struggle for moral authority is best approached through churches and chapels. They were its traditional voices and they still attracted considerable respect. The much criticised census of 1851 revealed that 62 per cent of the population attended church regularly. Since belief is usually more widespead than practice, churches formed a confident establishment. How evident is this in buildings?

What could be more confident than Ewan Christian's masterpiece – St Mark's, Belgrave Gate (1869)? It has everything a church should have: mystery, a sense of the holy and, in its spaces, details and furnishings, a reverent purposefulness. (Needless to say, it is due to be closed!) The exterior is rather French with a high apsidal east end, and the interior is rich and spacious, the dim light allowing the eye to pick out a high painted roof, squat polished granite piers and a huge liturgical space in the chancel, which has as its background an allegorical picture of Christ as the Lord of all labour. (The church had a Christian socialist tradition.) St Mark's is an ark of the faith: its purplish Charnwood slate facing, narrow windows and thrusting pinnacles and spires are all eloquent of strength, confidence and purpose. Indeed, so eloquent, that one may ask: why did the church have to be so visually insistent?

Impressive in a different though as insistent a way is S.S. Teulon's 1871 re-modelling of Holy Trinity, Regent Road, (happily, a church which is very much open.) This imaginative, though violently quirky architect clad Sydney Smirke's demure Regency box in a deep red brick (from a distance it looks bluish-purple) and erected, at the west end, an enormous raw and raucous steeple (flanked by two Fench pavilion roofs!) which sprouts shafts, gables, canopies, pinnacles and, at the top, an appropriately shrill weather-vane. Indeed, the whole west front is an exhilarating 'cock-a-doodle-do'. But again: why so loud?

Also impressive are two of the four Scott churches: St Andrew's (1860) and St Saviour's (1877). St Andrew's is strikingly original: a spacious, aisleless nave with a huge, over-arching wooden roof, a long apsidal chancel, very plain buttresses, simple windows and, covering much of the exterior, patterns in blue brick. The building breathes conviction; the architect knew exactly what a church should be like. St Saviour's is a fascinating blend of elegance and solidity. The great steeple (better than the Cathedral's?) soars above the roof ridge. Its style is early English, yet the great trunk of the church is romanesque and, by comparison, rougher and coarser. Its interior (the largest in the Diocese of Leicester) is splendid: polished granite piers shine in the huge cavernous crossing.

All those churches are by London architects but, at their best, the local men are worthy of such company. Joseph Goddard, Stockdale Harrison and F.W. Ordish all built interesting churches. Easily the best is Goddard's St John's, Clarendon Park Road of 1884. It is a great plain building with a little stone banding, plate tracery and, on its majestic roof, a slim lead spirelet. This wonderful roof and the amazing complexity of the interior – low double aisle passages supporting a gallery running round the entire church – give it the same assertive confidence as St Mark's, Holy Trinity and St Andrew's. Stockdale Harrison built two cheap churches: St Stephen's, East Park Road (1897) and St Thomas's, South Wigston (1892). They are simple brick buildings, yet not without surprises: both the interiors are aisleless, and St Thomas's has a bulky tower with big pinnacled buttresses and a lead spike. St Paul's, Kirby Road (1871) was Ordish's best work. It occupies a quite marvellous position on a ridge overlooking the City and, though bits of the design are jumbled, the big apsidal east end in which each bay has its own gable is wholly successful. The interior, because of its long established high church tradition, both looks and smells seriously devotional.

And these churches are not all. The Cathedral is Victorian, though its only good features are Raphael Brandon's steeple of 1860 and Pearson's south porch of 1896. St Peter's Highfields is by Street (1872); it is severe, lofty and thoughtfully detailed. The closed St John's (1853) – a splendid example of picturesque utility – is finely grouped and shows Scott's imaginative handling of different stones. St Michael and All Angels, Belgrave (George Vialls, 1885) has a portentous west end of big pinnacles and deeply set windows. The lavishly detailed St James the Greater of 1899 is the work of Henry Langton Goddard, son of Joseph. It is a puzzling building: plush Italianate in its overall conception, it has carved angels, which, on close inspection, turn out to be rather pale English maidens – anaemic daughters and granddaughters of Pre-Raphaelite stunners.

The religious and political power of Leicester non-conformists is well-known. The Baptists were both large and influential, the Methodists powerful in a quieter way and, though numerically tiny, the Quakers and Unitarians were at the centre of Leicester's social, political and economic life. Yet their buildings don't quite express the claims to power and authority evident in those of the Anglicans. Furthermore, it is a power that has passed. In addition to other demolished Baptist churches, the following have gone: Bond Street Congregational of 1821 where the heroic Mr Baines fought against the compulsory Church rate, Clyde Street Chapel and, also a Methodist building, the gothic Saxby Street.

Of those that remain, Victoria Road (1853), Melbourne Hall (1881), Curzon Street (1859), the Pork Pie Chapel (1845), Robert Hall (1900) and Clarendon Park Baptist (1893) and Congregational (1897) are all of interest, not least in the matter of style.

Architectural historians stress that Anglicans went for gothic and non-conformists for classical, but even in such a strong dissenting town as Leicester there are exceptions. John

Tarring's Victoria Road chapel, Redfern and Sawday's King Richard's Road (1881) and, in a free arts-and-crafts manner, James Tait's Clarendon Park Congregational Church are gothic, and Tait's Clarendon Park Baptist church, with its charming cupola, is Queen Anne. Tait also did (free of charge) the 1880 Sunday School Memorial Building in New Walk, and its style is free Tudor. Goddard's Melbourne Hall has gothic detailing though its shape, a great octagonal tub, is more akin to eighteenth century non-conformist chapels. Walter Brand's Robert Hall is turn-of-the-century free style and, in its metal work and leaded windows, almost art nouveau. Only Curzon Street, Joseph Hansom's 'Pork Pie' chapel and George Holme's charming York Street Chapel of 1866 are classical.

In terms of assertiveness and confidence, are these buildings too strident in their claims to moral authority? Their undoubted dominance of the townscape is perhaps a slightly desperate attempt to force the church upon the people. Holy Trinity is a wonderful building, but visually loud possible because it was in competition with another moral authority – education.

The dates are interesting. Forster's Education Act, which set up the School Boards, was passed in 1870; Holy Trinity was re-built in 1871, and St Mark's opened in 1872. The Leicester Board Schools competed visually with the churches. One of the visual functions of the churches was to dominate the townscape; even the smallish Church of the Martyrs (Ewan Christian 1889) is a powerful end-stop beyond the terraced houses in Ridley Street. The Board Schools, particularly those designed by Edward Burgess, attempted a similar authoritative statement. Take, for instance, Charnwood Street School. It was one of Burgess's earliest designs and remains one of his most impressive. Built on rising ground, it soars above the surrounding streets to proclaim the importance of education. Like many churches, it has a tower: a strong, secure-looking one above which rises above a rather baronial turret. Furthermore, its sheer size is expressive of its importance and, when first built in 1875, its bulk would have seemed even more assertive than it does to us today.

Charnwood Street is not the only school that offers a visual challenge to the churches. Ellis, with its big gables, towers above the houses in Bruin Street and forms a powerful end-stop to Ellis Avenue. Mantle Road School occupies a big site near the junction of Mantle, Tudor, Battenburg and Empire Roads, so that from many angles its handsome tower (a feature of so many of the schools) is visible. Two of the most spectacular are Belper Street and, the last of the Board Schools, Westcotes. Belper Street is a huge cubic form topped by a cupola. The sudden glimpse of it down Belper Street from the corner with Catherine Street, or from the railway going north to Nottingham, is the most visually stimulating sight in that part of Leicester. Westcotes is in many ways the grandest. Screened by trees, it stands on the busy junction of Upperton and Narborough Roads. It is tall, has huge windows, and from Noel Street magnificiently shuts out the view to the west. (Neither Belper Street nor Westcotes now function as schools.)

The size of these schools was a direct challenge to the church. No longer could people look to it alone as the only source of light and hope. These buildings enshrined a secular alternative, though it is only with the hindsight of the twentieth century, when education is almost entirely secular, that we can see this clearly. But a challenge they were, and one that was evident in two ways other than the sheer physical presence of the buildings: the juxtaposition of the schools with church buildings, and the style in which they were built.

The first point can best be seen in Clarendon Park. In 1889 St John the Baptist school was built in Clarendon Park Road. The architect, J.B. Everard, had a small site, so built a quite big, solidly massed school with tall windows and an attractive roof. Visually it was second only to the Church. But three years later came Avenue Road Board School. It occupies a big site between Clarendon Park Road, Lytton Road, Avenue Road and Lorne Road and, more to the point, it has a big tower with an open upper storey, which rises higher than the Anglican school no more than three hundred yards away. Imagine what the sight must have meant to the mid-1890s traveller entering Leicester on either the Welford or the London Road: he would see Church and School in visual competition over the open fields – with the School Board building reigning supreme.

The question of style is even more revealing. Churches favoured Gothic, so Gothic came to have ecclesiastical associations. Now though it is true that Burgess included gothic elements, his major stylistic source was Queen Anne, and that was the fashionable urban style of the 1870s, 1880s and 1890s. Moreover, it was thought of as the style of a refined and enlightened culture. In Arnold's words, it was the architecture of 'sweetness and light'. This sweetness and light is evident in the big symmetrically placed windows with their small, white painted, glazing bars, the careful use of brick mouldings, the rhythmic lines of decorated gables and the soaring towers and cupolas. Here was culture – sweetness and light – for everyone: it was a form of secular salvation expressed in the most sophisticated style of the day.

There were other architectural challenges to the authority of the Church. Throughout the century a number of buildings spoke of the growing influence of municipal power. To the County Asylum, prison and workhouse, should be added other Leicester landmarks. The cemetery on Welford Road, opened 1849, was the work of the Corporation. Although its gothic chapels, the work of Hamilton and Medland, have gone, it remains an essentially Victorian scene: celtic crosses, Greek memorials, renaissance tombs and some art nouveau lettering and metal work. An even bigger area is taken up by the Towers, a purpose-built mid-Victorian mental hospital. It stands on the brow of a tree-lined hill, and its style is what architectural historians called 'Jacobethan'. Other hospitals include Beaumont Smith's children's ward in the Royal Infirmary of 1888 (Queen Anne), Blackwell and Thomson's Isolation hospital on Groby Road (also Queen Anne) and the earlier but historically important Freake's ground isolation hospital, which was built as part of the campaign against smallpox. Related to hospitals were the baths. Most of the Victorian ones have disappeared, an exception being Cossington Street of 1897 which stands alongside the branch library and the recreation ground. There are also branch libraries in Narborough Road (Stockdale Harrison, 1888), Garendon Street (Millican, 1884) and Clarendon Park (A.H. Hind 1896). Other public parks include Spinney Hill and the extensive Abbey Park, laid out in 1881.

The best expression of secular triumph is the Town Hall. One of the most refreshing things about Leicester in the last twenty years has been the growing awareness that, in this lovely building, the citizens of Leicester have something both architecturally special and characteristically local. The style, based no doubt on Eden Nesfield's Kimnel Park, is a gentle, domestic Queen Anne. It is light, airy, friendly and modest and expresses another kind of confidence – not the confidence of the church, but a growing assurance of the ascendancy in ordinary people's lives of municipal influence.

OPPOSITE LEFT: St Mark's is a masterpiece with an uncertain future. Its great, soaring spire expresses the firm assurance of Victorian religion. Its second vicar, Lewis Donaldson, helped to lead the march of unemployed from Leicester to London in 1903, and his successor, Linwood Wright, invited the Corporation to see a pageant in the Church and then preached about the folly of pulling down houses in his parish. With the reorganisation of parishes, St Mark's may be closed. RIGHT: Leicester's most vigorous and visually loud church: Holy Trinity was considered too modest, so in 1871 S.S. Teulon, the most gifted of those idiosyncratic Victorian architects called 'rogues', clad it in brick and erected a huge steeple, which bristles with details and is flanked by two French Pavilion roofs! BELOW: The Christian Socialist theology preached in St Mark's by Lewis Donaldson, who is said to have formulated the phrase often attributed to Charles Gore, that 'Christianity is the religion of which socialism is the practice', found visual expression in the mural in the apse – The Triumph and Apotheosis of Labour – painted in 1910 by J. Eadie Reid.

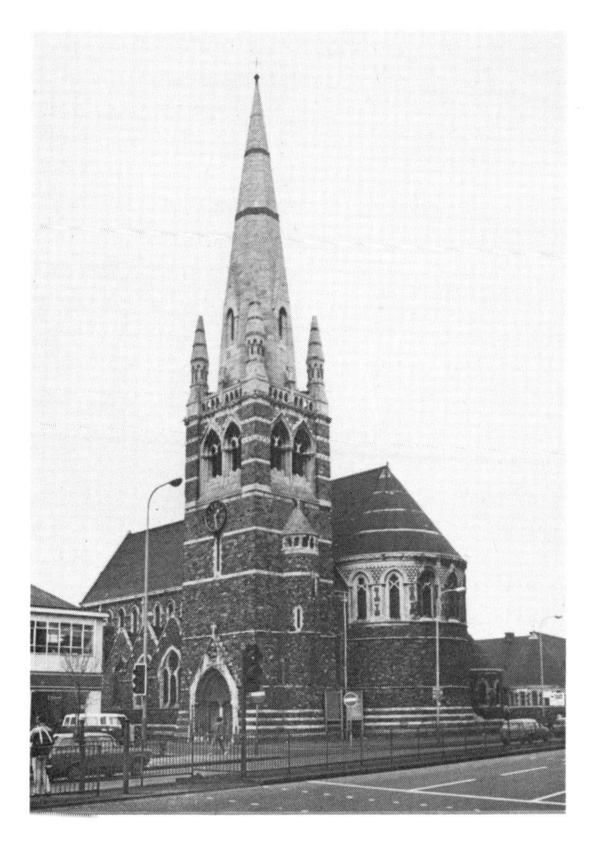

LEFT: St Andrew's, Jarrom Street, built in 1860 by Sir George Gilbert Scott. RIGHT: Scott built four new churches in Leicester of which the first was St John's. BELOW: St John the Baptist, Clarendon Park Road (1884) is the work of a local architect — Joseph Goddard.

ABOVE LEFT: Victoria Road Church was built on the corner of London Road and Victoria Road in 1853 and though the latter has been called University Road for some years, it still retains its original name. The Baptists built it; and the architect was a Londoner, John Tarring. It is now the Seventh Day Adventist Church. RIGHT: Clarendon Park Congregational Church, on the corner of London and Springfield Road, was built in 1885, (architect, James Tait). One of its earlier ministers, P.T. Forsyth is thought by some to be the most creative British theologian of this century. To-day it is one of the leading Congregational Churches not to join with the Presbyterians to form the United Reform Church. BELOW LEFT: A house of 1888 by Arthur Wakerley and Goddard's Melbourne Hall of 1881. RIGHT: The secular Hall is a meeting place for committed unbelievers, built in 1881. The carved heads in their own non-religious niches are of humanitarian worthies: Socrates, Jesus, Voltaire, Tom Paine and Robert Owen.

LEFT: This spiky Gothic building was for many years both Elim Pentecostal Church and a hardware shop. On Ruding Road was the church entrance; on Narbourough Road, there were tin baths and wire netting out on the pavement. It was originally built by the Harris family, who lived in the big house called 'Westcotes,' as a school; the architects were Henry and Joseph Goddard. RIGHT: Stoneygate School stands back from London Road. It was built, probably by Henry Goddard, father of the more famous Joseph, in 1859 as Franklin's School. Later it was known (and still is to many people) as Rudd's School. BELOW: Charnwood Street School is one of the earliest of the Board Schools and, happily, it is still in use.

LEFT: Belper Street Board School, designed by Edward Burgess in 1887, rises confidently above the streets of terraced houses like a church. RIGHT: A temple to education: Mantle Road Board School of 1896 has, like many other Board Schools, the characteristics of a church or chapel. BELOW: Medway Street Board School of 1884 has a row of plain gables overlooking the playground on the Medway Street side, and big windows and decorative brickwork in the gables (sweetness and light) on the section facing Tichborne Street. The solid purposefulness of the former and the pride of the latter reflect the importance laid upon education in the late Victorian period. Such ideas were shared by the liberal and Quaker architect, Edward Burgess.

LEFT: The last of the Board Schools, Westcotes, designed by Edward Burgess shortly befor the abolition of the Schools Boards in 1902. RIGHT: The nineteenth was the century of institutions: schools, hospitals, barracks, prisons, workhouses and asylums. Leicester's mental hospital, The Towers, was built in 1869 by F.L. Stephens, the Borough Surveyor. BELOW: The branch libraries on Narborough Road, built in 1888 by Stockdale Harrison.

LEFT: This Gatehouse, alone amid allotments near Fosse and Groby Road, was built in 1872 as part of the Borough Fever and Smallpox Hospital. Under Dr William Johnston, it was used for a scheme of smallpox treatment later applied worldwide. RIGHT: Water Board Office of 1865 by Shenton and Baker. BELOW: Late Victorian guides mentioned 'The Home', (for the reformation of fallen women), but not where it was! It stands on the corner of Stoneygate and Aber Roads. The architect, Beaumont Smith, was also architect to the Royal Infirmary.

ABOVE The Town Hall in 1876, shortly before it was opened. To the right in Horsefair Street is the Theatre Royal, built by William Parsons in 1836. BELOW: The Welford Road Cemetery opened in 1849 and was divided into consecrated ground for Anglicans and, because they were politically the most powerful group, the highest ground unconsecrated for the non-conformists.

Leicester is not a City of fine statues, so for public memorials the sight-seer has to go to Welford Road Cemetery.Though there are no large ones (the biggest – the Turner Mausoleum – was demolished about fifteen years ago), a pleasing variety of styles can be found: ABOVE LEFT: the Celtic Cross; RIGHT: Renaissance; BELOW LEFT: Gothic; CENTRE: Art Nouveau and RIGHT: Moorish.

ABOVE: In any large city 'the tech' has a special place in the hearts of many people. It was an opportunity to better oneself, and the evening class offered the prospect of certificates, diplomas or, in a word not heard much these days, 'letters'. This is the original building of the art and tech, built in 1896 to a design by Everard and Pick. BELOW: Morland Avenue was laid out by Stockdale Harrison in 1904. He built many of the houses including the first five on the left.

The Edwardian Era

At its best Edwardian Leicester has grace and ease. In commercial building there is thoughtfulness, fun and a dignity that manages not to be pompous, and its domestic work is homely yet sophisticated, spacious without being impracticable and weighty and solid without being overbearing. It has much in common with the architecture of the 1890s, though the one thing it often lacks that Victorian buildings had in abundance is 'fizz'.

Perhaps the 'fizz' isn't there because the pressure was easing off. Edwardian Leicester did grow, but the rate of expansion was less than in the previous two or three decades. Of course, many of the areas of Victorian growth continued to be infilled. In addition, there were developments on the edges of the town. For instance, the roads between Evington and Kimberley Roads – Dashwood Road, Draper Street, Devana Road among others – were built, and further south there was building on Stoughton Drive North. On the west side of the town, building continued on and near Fosse Road, Hinckley Road and Narborough Road, so in 1908 D.H. Lawrence was able to visit his aunt at 20 Dulverton Road. Perhaps the best way to enjoy the flavour of Edwardian Leicester is to consider three small developments: Morland Avenue, Sykefield Avenue and Humberstone Garden Suburb.

Morland Avenue, built from 1904 onwards, is largely the work of Stockdale Harrison. Most of the houses are comfortably domestic and spacious without being unmanageable: the roofs are big, there is sparing use of hanging tile, many are rendered with roughcast, the windows all have small panes, there are good solid chimney stacks and inside, thoughtfully designed details – art nouveau bell fittings, thin balusters on the staircases and, occasionally, decorative plaster work. The road is lined with thin silver birches, and that, somehow, is right: they form a delicate screen, are leafy without being thick and woody, and present an image of a refined yet quite rural existence.

Sykefield Avenue, between Westcotes Drive and Ashleigh Road, deserves notice because it has three contrasting houses. On the corner with Upperton Road there is a 1910 block by Stockdale Harrison, with roughcast rendering and good chimneys. It has a healthy air about it; one could imagine its residents going on long hikes into the Charnwood Forests or going by bike to Foxton Locks or Rutland villages. On the opposite side is a red brick block of 1906 by Everard and Pick which is distinctly rural, even arts-and-crafts, in origin. Its cottagey look is created by overhanging eaves, a big roof and the easy rhythm of the frontage. But most interesting of all is the house on the corner with Westcotes Drive. Here we have just a touch of Charles Rennie Mackintosh: a house designed by Charles Kempson for John Russell Frears in 1902. The Westcotes Drive front is not interesting, though the fruity art nouveau glass is attractive, but the side onto Sykefield, particularly the way the chimney is treated to create a skyline of curving and angular forms (and the shafted windows), is so striking as to be almost un-Leicester. Its freedom and ease, so characteristic of Edwardian architecture at its best, is something to be relished.

The Edwardian world was one that knew itself to be poised between the town and the country. They lived in towns but wanted, if they could afford it, space, greenery and architectural remembrances of rural life. Such desires were often strengthened by idealistic visions of community life. It is, therefore, not surprising that the garden suburb idea attracted them – space, trees, shrubs, long gardens with big vegetable patches, cottage/style houses and a sense of communal endeavour. Humberstone Garden Suburb, started in 1907, is Leicester's contribution to the garden suburb movement. It is small, comprising just five aptly named roads – Laburnum Road, Lilac Avenue, Fern Rise, Chestnut Avenue and Rosebank Way between Keyham Lane and Netherhall Road. The cottages, designed by George Hern, are spaciously set, eight to an acre, in a layout by Parker and Unwin, chief designers of Letchworth – doyen of garden cities. The gardens are long, the cottages gabled and covered with roughcast, and in the centre there is a little green, a church and a row of shops.

Edwardian domestic architecture is characterised by a free use of many of the vernacular elements introduced by the Victorians. Much the same can be said of the churches. Gone are the abrasive qualities seen in St Andew's and Holy Trinity; instead, buildings are mild, unobtrusive and thoughtfully detailed.

The Unitarian church on Narborough Road (now Elim Pentecostal) was designed in 1901 by Charles Kempson. It is free perpendicular with overhanging eaves, curved buttresses that emerge from the lean-to aisles and coping stones that give a gentle, free-flowing look to the building. All Souls, which was designed in 1904 by G.F. Bodley, is quiet, restrained and would be merely bland were it not for the contemplative interior which features tall, narrow side passages (hardly aisles) and the large grey reredos before which hangs a silver altar light. St Alban's is a simple yet engaging building designed in 1905 by H.H. Thompson. From a distance it looks gothic, but the details are handled so freely it would be a mistake to classify it in purely stylistic terms. The best feature is the gently rippling coping over the aisle: it runs smoothly, coming to a point at the division of each bay of the building. Like Kempson's church it has overhanging eaves. Everard and Pick's St Philip's, Evington Road (1909) is the most arts-and-crafts of them all, particularly its interior with big pointed arches in brick rising from the floor, and its charming light fittings.

Two charity buildings should be mentioned: the Cripple's Guild (1910) and the YMCA (1899 – 1900). A.E. Sawday's Cripple's Guild (now the Guild for the Physically Handicapped) in Colton Street is a pleasing exercise in free form, with attractive stonework in sweeping curves and a big hood above the central door. The YMCA, though strictly speaking Victorian, is in the triumphantly loud Baroque idiom that was popular in the 1890s and 1900s. It is the work of Draper and Walters who, given a strategic site near the railway station, produced a building that no young man new to Leicester could avoid seeing. If they made the hundred yards down London Road without being lured into a pub, they would find security within this busily fronted haven.

Baroque was an accepted commercial style. Given that it is the architecture of power – the deep shadows cast by attached columns and rustication eloquently express a building's strength and force – it was appropriately used for banks as in the case of St Martin's, Barclay's on Horsefair Street and the smaller and stylistically freer Stamford, Spalding and Boston Banking Company in Gallowtree Gate, later to become Barclay's and now Top Man. Both these latter buildings have interesting carving. Sawday, who designed Barclay's Bank in 1900, was no doubt responsible for the languid figures above the doorway (they seem to suggest a profession slightly older than banking), and Stockdale Harrison in 1907 provided some wonderful heavy-eyed maidens(?) which overlook Gallowtree Gate. Perhaps the associations of wealth and power made Baroque the obvious style for Goddard's re-building, in 1898, of the News Reading Room on the corner of Belvoir Street and Granby Street. And on the opposite side of the road is the most eloquent flourish of all: a huge Baroque corner tower in the style of a Thomas Archer steeple. It was done in 1898 by Amos Hall for the Grand Hotel.

But there were other commercial styles. In 1903 Stockdale Harrison mixed Baroque and vernacular elements in the rightly named Grand Clothing Hall on the corner of High Street and Bond Street. The design of the facades is pretty stunning (look at the deeply set round headed window overlooking High Street), but more amazing is the roof surmounted by a huge lantern which serves no apparent purpose than that of entertainment. More vernacular, and certainly less heated, is Charles Kempson's civilized design for Hopewell's. Built in 1901, it forms a successful corner at the top end of a now much truncated St Nicholas Street. The same thoughtful use of wood is to be found in Market Street where Stoyell's shop, now alas shorn of its ground floor, sold linen from 1910. Two shops in Braunstone Gate are of interest: Frank Jones's Tudor style facade done in 1902 for Frank Gadsby, and Langley and Baine's great, if a little strained corner piece where the Gate meets Western Road. It is a bold composition in stone, brick (glazed and unglazed) in a sort of free Baroque style. Even freer is the almost dateless Morgan Squire's (now Rackham's) which, in its white stone, is an eye-catcher when looking up Horsefair Street. It was done by Everard and Pick in 1907. And, for a bit of sheer fun in the shopping world, have a look at what was Butler's the Chemists on the corner of High Street and Cart's Lane. Sawday's design of 1903 is entertaining, particularly the corner entrance, but the most jolly features are the ceramic panels facing the High Street, one of which advertises a mixture called Sea Breeze which, judging from the image of the ship at sea, made one's tummy light, buoyant and ready for anything.

Yet two pieces of commercialism have visual pre-eminence: Arthur Wakerley's Turkey Café of 1900 and Amos Hall's Silver Arcade of 1899. They are very different: the café is covered in beautifully pale and subtle Doulton tiles, designed by F. Neatby, whereas the Arcade sprouts stonework outside and within, has plaster friezes of merry little dancing boys. As far as style goes, the Café is decidedly Eastern, while the Arcade sports almost every kind of Baroque detailing – broken pediments, attached columns and finials. Yet they have one thing in common – fun.

Fun has left its mark in other ways: the first twenty years of the century provided Leicester with a number of good buildings, the aim of which was to provide leisure, entertainment and uplift. The most important one is the De Monfort Hall, built in 1913 to the designs of Shirley Harrison. Until the recent building of the concert hall in Nottingham, it was the only large hall in the East Midlands, and what is more, it made Leicester famous. To many East Midlanders Leicester means just one thing – the De Montfort Hall. And it even earned the praise of Sir Thomas Beecham, who called it one of the finest concert halls in the country.

Another kind of entertainment could be enjoyed at the Cameo Cinema in the High Street, which was originally built as the Arcadia Electric Theatre by the Birmingham firm of Ward and Bell in 1910. Although it now functions as an amusement arcade, the thrill of the days of the silver screen, focussed in that word, so modern, so daring, so alluring, 'Electric', is still there in the stuccoed entrance section. Descending even lower down an imaginary entertainment scale, we find what is probably the best pub building in Leicester – Stockdale Harrison's arts-and-crafts Saracen's Head (1904) in Hotel Street. It has all the right features: beautiful brickwork, a good doorway, brackets supporting the guttering and, its crowning feature, a big Swithland slate roof. And in 1901 A.E. Sawday built the main cricket pavilion at Grace Road. Finally, there is a good, simple building which combines entertainment and seriousness: W.K. Bedingfield's Adult School of 1911 in Western Road. Leicester people were ardent self-improvers, so the evening class was both useful and pleasurable.

The effect of the First World War on Leicester is dificult to assess. It resulted in one permanent building – the Junior Training Hall – which we know as the Granby Halls. And in Holbrook Road the Knighton Memorial Hall, built in 1919 by the firm of Stockdale Harrison, is an eloquent farewell to a past era, designed, as it is, in a very Edwardian style. Of the people themselves, it can be said that they were proud of the resilience the 4th Leicesters showed at the Hohenzollern Redoubt: but who can (or should) dare to assess what effects the countless deaths of those four years had upon the town. Stories still circulate which show a little of the terrible impact it had. One will suffice. When James Went, headmaster since 1877 of Wyggeston Boys' School, heard of the death of Alan Mason, his most talented pupil, the old man wept.

A collective expression of grief was made in 1926 with the building of Lutyens's massive arch of remembrance in Victoria Park. It is different from the emotionally fraught memorial to the dead of the South African War that stands in the Town Hall Square. Its sculptor, Crossland McClure, released emotion in the agonised and contorted figures; Lutyens's arch controls and transforms a town's grief into an eloquent expression of loss. Some think it too triumphalist, but that is a grave misunderstanding. Stand one evening and face the City as it is framed by the arch and consider the shape – a huge, aching void, which plangently tells of a people whose heart has been wrenched out.

This rural terrace, designed in 1906 by Everard and Pick is in Sykefield Avenue. Their self-conscious cottagey look still appeals to the eye made sore by high rise flats, stained concrete and urban motorways. It is not surprising that this reticent, arts and crafts architecture is making a come-back.

LEFT: The house of John Russell Frears, the biscuit manufacturer, on the corner of Westcotes Drive and Sykefield Avenue, is the most striking, even the most daring, piece of Edwardian domestic architecture in Leicester. Charles Kempson built it in 1902. RIGHT: The house of Shirley Harrison — 'Four Gables' — was built on Elms Road in 1910. BELOW: The north side of the High Street was newly built after it was widened in 1902.

Theatreland
TO LET

Hopewells international furniture
FOR SALE OR TO LET
P
Cathedral

OPPOSITE ABOVE: The Silver Arcade, designed by Amos Hall in 1899: How much better it is than modern shopping centres! BELOW: Hopewell's, designed by Charles Kempson in 1901, is one of Leicester's best Edwardian shops. ABOVE LEFT: A successful piece of Edwardian commericialism which still looks fresh and lively: Everard and Pick's building for Morgan Squire's (now Rackham's) proudly occupies an important City centre site on the corner of Horsefair and Hotel Street. The original shop, part of which still remains further along Hotel Street, was founded by Samuel Squire. RIGHT: The aptly named Grand Clothing Hall, built in 1903 by Stockdale Harrison, dominates the east end of High Street with its somewhat imperious lantern. It was built for a local clothing firm, Hart and Levy. Sir Israel Hart, an active member of the Jewish community, gave the fountain in the Town Hall Square. To the left is the office of wine merchants W.A. Gilby, built in 1903 by G. Lawton Brown, and beyond, to the right, is the extraordinary spike surmounting Tyler's shop, also a 1903 building by Morton Cowdell. BELOW LEFT: High Street's equivalent of the Crystal Palace: Arthur Wakerley's Singer building of 1902 is dominated by a huge glass barrel vault. CENTRE: Arthur Wakerley's liking for tile is evident in the exotic orientalism of his Turkey Café (1900). The tiles were the design of F. Neatby of Doulton. RIGHT: Frank Jones designed this Tudor shop for Frank Gadsby in 1902. Gadsby's has long been the leading art gallery in Leicester.

ABOVE: The De Montfort Hall was built in 1913 to a design by Shirley Harrison, son of Stockdale Harrison. It is a fine concert hall with an impressive exterior. The gardens are always maintained to a high standard. The local story that it was only a contemporary structure is quite false, being based on a confusion between the Hall and a short-lived building erected for a meeting of the British Association. LEFT: The Palace on Belgrave Gate was designed in 1900 by Frank Matcham. RIGHT: A world that has lost its heart: the aching void of Sir Edwin Lutyens's arch expresses not the triumph of victory but the grief of communal bereavement.

The Way We Live Now

For about the first sixty years of this century Leicester was visually stable, though there were some changes. The City (it was designated as such in 1919) grew as outlying land was bought up for building and, in response to changing architectural fashions, new work reflected a number of idioms – the art deco of some factories and cinemas, in the 'way' Roads (Highway, Byway, Midway etc), the English liking for faintly Tudor – little gables and black and white timbering – semi-detached houses. Yet stability was maintained because, by later standards, there was little demolition. Photographs taken in the 1940s and 1950s show a city which had lots of Victorian shop fronts, Victorian theatres, Victorian churches, hundreds of terraced houses within easy walking distance of the centre, streets following their medieval courses and at least one case of a medieval house – the St Mary de Castro Rectory. The texture of the City – its small-scale intimacy and busy variety – began to change after the Second World War, but was not seriously coarsened until the large-scale demolition of the hubristic 1960s. The 1970s were less savage, and, so far, the 1980s even milder, but even so the rate of change is, compared with earlier decades, considerable.

One way of representing change is to recall what has gone. Here is a short list: St Luke's, St Hilda's, St Leonard's Emmanuel Baptist, Archdeacon Lane Baptist, Saxby Street Methodist, the Temperance Hall, the Bell Hotel, Everard's Brewery, the Theatre Royal, the Consanguinitarium, the Fielding-Johnson factories, the *Leicester Mail* Office, Marshall and Snelgrove's, Simpkin and James's, the Picture House, Bow Bridge Works, the Wyvern Hotel, the Hotel Victory, the Pack Horse Hotel, Waterloo House (the best house in New Walk), Lord's Place, and many of the bridges built to conduct the Central Line into and out of Leicester. And those are just the buildings. Just think of the streets: what happened to Highcross Street, Southgates and Hastings Street? Just think of how the advance towards each other of the Infirmary and the Polytechnic has left nothing in between but a few factories, the magnificent St Andrew's and the modern estate. Elsewhere, the Wharf Street area has all but disappeared, demoliton in Highfields has made room for a streaky concrete wedge – the St Peter's Estate. West End roads have swallowed up many of the streets between Hinckley Road and King Richard's Road and, most recently of all, a genuine and characteristically bitty vernacular terrace in St Martin's has given way to the mass-produced vernacular of the 1980s.

If, however, one wants an alternative to a requiem one can ask two questions: what impact has demolition had? What are the forces which, over the decades, have shaped the Leicester in which we now live?

The first question can be answered quite briefly. What has gone is intimacy, bittiness, surprise small-scale humanity and a likeable, though sometimes shabby, provincial purposefulness. At one time there were little streets of houses no more than two storeys high, corner shops with painted advertisements for pills or tobacco, non-conformist chapels with names such as Salem or Ebenezer, clattering hosiery factories, unobtrusive pubs and, adding scale, cinemas with ceramic facing tiles and arrow motifs in the metalwork of doors and windows. What has replaced that Leicester is blander, cleaner, more rational and dully national and international in style. What, for instance, is typically Leicester about say, the St Peter's Estate or the Haymarket Centre?

The forces that have made the Leicester in which we live are transport, high-rise building and the local authority. With the exception of the second, which is an entirely post-1960s contribution, the forces are not new. The first is the factor that has controlled the town from the very start, while the third was making itself felt in the nineteenth century.

As early as 1902 High Street was widened. This involved the demolition of many buildings, including Lord's Place, and the building of some enjoyable showy Edwardian shops, the most striking of which – Arthur Wakerley's Singer Building of 1902 – is full of imperial confidence with its symbols of Empire – (an elephant, a kangaroo) – and its glass barrel roof, which is reminiscent of the Crystal Palace. The broad thoroughfare created by the widening might have re-asserted the original Roman west-east axis of the town, but subsequent attempts to relieve traffic congestion reverted to the medieval north-south one.

From 1929 Charles Street was widened in an attempt to carry north-south traffic through the town, without clogging up Granby Street and threatening the position of the Clock Tower. In the memories of Leicester's more senior generation the opening of Charles Street in 1932 was (and is) an important event. It is a pity, therefore, that it is not more interesting. At the Northampton Street end it was given a grand entrance by Noel Hill's Police Station of 1933, and on the corner of Rutland Street there are the municipal offices which, visually speaking, are now coming into their own, but otherwise the buildings are neither interesting nor distinctively local. And what is more, its atmosphere is not a local one. People always seem to be in a hurry, the shops seem a little out of place, and the offices are anonymous.

But even greater changes were yet to come; under the influence of City Planning Officer Konrad Smigielski (the man who has visually transformed Leicester more than anybody else, with the possible exception of Henry II and the Roman architect who laid out Ratae) a great road system – St Margaret's Way, Burley's Way and Southgate began to be imposed upon the northern and western parts of the medieval town. This meant demolition on a large scale: Thornton Lane, Harvey Lane, Redcross Street, Bakehouse Lane, Bridge Street (and known as West Bridge Street) and Applegate all went. One name survived: a stretch of Highcross Street has recently been re-named Applegate, in spite of the fact that it is at least a hundred yards from its original course. In the place of these streets – all of which had medieval courses – there is the underpass and the Holiday Inn.

Since then the new Leicestershire authority has been responsible for roads. The work in the West End and the attempts to complete the inner ring (an inappropriately Wagnerian concept for modest Leicester), have resulted in more tarmac and less character. Visually speaking, we have yet to learn how to live with the motor car. Our Victorian forebears found their railways more picturesque companions.

Leicester went 'high-rise' in the early 1960s. The visual transformation is evident from the 'heights' surrounding the City. From the M1 as it curves through Narborough, the University stands starkly out against the sky. From the A50 as it descends past Gilroes Cemetery it is again visible, along with the Cardinal Telephone Exchange on Humberstone Road, the Post Office building in Charles Street and, on the other side of the City, the twin towers of Rowlatt's Hill. From the east, on the gentle hills that lead out to Barkby, the tall buildings are again noticeable, with the Rowlatt's Hill development the most prominent. Since they are so much of the scene, it's appropriate to think about what they are like as buildings, and the contribution they make to Leicester.

They vary. Some are dull, even inert; others are good of their kind, and one or two have character. The tower blocks on St Peter's Estate are forbidding, largely because they do not remotely look as if they could be homes. Perhaps some residents find they are, in which case their function must belie their appearance. The Cardinal Telephone Exchange is better, as is Epic House, home of Radio Leicester. One of the most interesting is St John's House – a building of bluish brick not unlike the colours of the nearby church – which, unlike many tall buildings, is thoughtfully moulded and grouped. Also interestingly moulded are the two blocks for single persons by John Middleton – Elizabeth House by the station and the iceberg-like block on Oxford Street. They are part of a (laudable) attempt to encourage people back into the City centre, thirty years after demolition drove them out. My own favourite is the GPO building on Charles Street: austere and almost clinical in conception, it has an elegant form and makes a good end-stop to Charles Street.

But what contribution do they actually make? That is a very difficult question to answer, because the people of Leicester largely ignore them. We certainly notice them from a distance and, occasionally looking up a familiar street, we are surprised to find the sun has been shut out. More generously, we might admit that they contribute scale. But the mental picture most of us have of our City does not include them, possibly because they are simply not characteristic of Leicester. For instance, how many of them are in red brick or brick at all? It is not surprising that in our heads (and cities and towns exist there as well as on the ground) we do not often given them a place. The high-rise block is too American a concept for the English to adopt as their own. The only possible exception in Leicester is Welford Place, not because of its architecture, but because we are governed from it. Perhaps we may come to look upon it as 'ours'. But I doubt it.

The Welford Road offices bring us to the third element that shapes present-day Leicester – the local authority. If it is legitimate to read the history of nineteenth century Leicester as a struggle, albeit an often undeclared one, between two moral authorities – the church and the municipal authority – it follows that the twentieth century should be regarded as the triumph of the latter. Everywhere we look we see the visible presence of our political masters. The Welford Place Civic Centre was not purpose-built (it was a speculative building designed in 1971 by Newman, Levinson and partners), but I frequently wonder about the kind of image the Council wanted to project to itself when they bought these two utilitarian monoliths – dominance, clinical efficiency, the allseeing presence of civic power?

More evidence of civic power can be seen in the tower blocks of the Polytechnic (always nearer the hearts of Leicester people than the still somehow remote University), the tower blocks on the St Matthew's, St Peter's and Rowlatt's Hill Estate, the quite splendid circular libraries of St Barnabas and Southfields (both the work of Symington, Prince and Pike in 1937 and 1939 respectively), the De Montfort Hall, the St Margaret's baths, the fine, spacious public parks (Leicester does seem to have more than most cities), the schools (though for an expression of quite astonishing pride in public education you have to look at the County Upper schools, particularly Wreake Valley – designed in 1967) and, bang in the heart of the City, the Haymarket Centre of 1971. Lest that list sounds harshly critical (it was not meant to be) it should be added that the clean-up campaign has quite transformed Leicester's surface, the renewal scheme is bringing whole areas back from the prospect of certain demolition, and the planning department, with the odd slip, has a sensitive and conscientious attitude to the conservation of what the 1960s has left us.

The area in which the power of the local authority is most evident is that of housing. A third of the accommodation in the City is owned by the Council. A glance at a map of Leicester will reveal an almost complete ring of council estates from Eyres Monsell and Saffron Lane in the south-west through to Braunstone in the west, New Parks in the north west, Stocking Farm in the north, Northfields in the north-east and, to the east and south-east Coleman, Goodwood, Nether Hall and Rowlatt's Hill. There are gaps, the biggest being the wedge occupied by Evington and Knighton, but not many. And within that ring there are St Matthew's, St Andrew's and St Peter's Estate.

Council housing started in 1900 in Winifred Street. The buildings are still there – solid, slightly formal and not over-friendly blocks, with regularly spaced windows and communal staircases disposed round some welcome grass and trees. These were the work of T.H. Fosbrooke, an architect in private practice. In the early days of council housing and other civic works this was not unusual. Another characteristic of Winifred Street was that it was small scale. Such modesty was maintained when council housing started on a larger scale after the First World War. In 1921 an attractive terrace of forty houses was built in Kimberley Road. They are thoughtfully designed with moulded doorways and sash windows. Even the early work on Coleman Road was small: one plan shows just twenty-eight homes.

But all that changed with the coming of the Council Estate. Quite soon there were three: Braunstone, Saffron Lane and Coleman. Braunstone is the most well known of these early Estates. Its history is quite a complex one, consisting of three phases. The first was a quite modest development – the Wyggeston Charity Estate – just off the Narborough Road. The names of the roads tell their own story – Sweetbriar Road, Lavender Road and Gaddesby Avenue. The intimate plan of these streets and the cottagey styles further enhanced by the variety of house-types, indicate that the Garden City movement lies behind the scheme: residents were to enjoy good living standards in pleasant surroundings, which blended the freedom of the country with amenities of the town. The second phase was much more substantial. Councillors Gooding and Hallam negotiated the compulsory purchase of the Winstanley Estate, and with Lanchester as consultant, Fyffe of the housing department designed the houses. Their thinking was still rural: there were to be open spaces, grass verges, trees, and the roads (apart from those named after the benefactors – Gooding Avenue and Hallam Crescent East) were again redolent of the countryside – New Fields Avenue, Folville Rise and Waltham Avenue. And not just the countryside of the artisan: Audley End and Harlaxton Street make much bigger claims. The third phase came in 1936 when over six hundred houses were built in what became Braunstone North, to which a further four hundred were added in 1937. The styles of these later houses are still unmistakably vernacular and rural – brick, pebble dash, little gables, paling fences enclosing little gardens which, no doubt, were meant to be planted with hollyhocks and sunflowers to frame the small-paned windows. Whether or not Fyffe was conscious of it, what he was doing was updating the estate cottages that Butterfield had built for the Winstanleys of Braunstone Hall in 1858 and 1859. The parallel between the Winstanleys building cottages for their 'Estate' workers and the Council using a similar style for their tenants has intriguing political overtones.

Braunstone has long attracted the interests of historians and sociologists but it was not alone in being a big post-First World War development. Saffron Lane was also large. In 1923 there were two plans to build ninety-six and a hundred and four houses. And again the lay-out and style is rural. Just look at the delightful Cottager's Close off Stonesby Avenue, where pleasingly varied houses overlook a big open space. Building began there in 1928.

Styles changed. Braunstone, Coleman, Northfields, Saffron Lane and the small Freake's Estate are visually akin, but later developments reflected subsequent ideas of what a house should be. Some have been distinctly odd. St Matthew's Estate (1965) has such a complex ground plan that some of its residents get lost in it; St Andrew's is more intimate but is so turned in upon itself as to be rather forbidding to the outsider and, what is more, its exposed concrete has not improved with age. Grimmest of all is St Peter's. There is something horribly appropriate about the fact that many of the streets have solar system names – Neptune and Pluto being two – because the townscape is as alien as a distant planet. Recently, though, the spirit of Braunstone in the 1920s has returned. The latest work on Rowlatt's Hill is in the new (!) vernacular style: big tiles on the roof, brick, roughcast, wooden porches, round headed windows and a sweeping layout in which two and three storeyed houses happily blend. Take a walk up Balderstone Drive for a taste of the latest thinking. Some people called it Noddyland, Toy Town or Trumpton. Certainly the scale is a little odd, but the houses themselves are so much closer to what most people think a house ought to be. If you are in doubt cast your eyes up the hill to the two huge towers.

The latest area of housing – Beaumont Leys – is an almost entirely separate township to the north-west of Leicester. Planned in 1967, it could have been quite awful: the original scheme included high-rise blocks which, thankfully, were excluded in the sane revision of the plan in 1978. Beaumont Leys again shows the controlling presence of the local authority but, unlike the Estates discussed above, it is a mixed private and public development. Visually it is not unlike Milton Keynes, in that there is a contrast between sweeping roads and little clusters of houses, built round closes, where the motor car is catered for, but not welcomed. There is a bewildering variety of styles and materials – dark red brick, beige brick, roughcast, weather boarding, pitched, mono-pitched and almost flat roofs – which can be a bit much, but on balance the rather desperate striving for individuality is more welcome than rigid uniformity. The openness of the roads, the numerous mature trees, the variations in level (some houses are built in what I would call dells) give it all (again!) a country feeling.

And that, surely, is deliberate. There is a hollow filled with buildings in dark red brick with mono-pitched roofs called Barleycroft, which has a pub called The Meadows. Other road names are Great Meadow Road, Little Barley Close, Keeper's Walk and an industrial estate called Gorse Hill. Most notorious of all is a television advertisement for the shopping centre which starts with pictures of bunny rabbits frolicking on the edge of a wood! This shopping centre, heralded by four tall flagpoles, is appropriately folksy: there are lots of hipped roofs, enclosed and open shopping areas, one change in level and at a crossing little signposts directing one to the car parks, each of which is numbered but which, for those of us who have already sunk to the state of sub-numeracy, also bear animal emblems – a fox, a badger, an owl, a squirrel and the ubiquitous bunny. Here the Leisure Centre is being built and, next to it, the Ecumenical Centre which if you cannot even count, you will be unlikely to recognise as the church. One only hopes that, when completed, it will not be another of the mono-pitched roof ones, which have appeared elsewhere in the City – a sign, perhaps, that the church is preaching an attenuated transcendence.

Yet Beaumont Leys is much nicer than it could have been. We should be thankful that the fashions of one age – the 1960s – have been countered by a civic power which, as well as being in touch with 1980s fashions is also more in touch with what makes a humane environment.

ABOVE: A stable townscape: the centre of Leicester from the tower of St John's, Albion Street in the post-war decade. There are no highrise buildings, so the skyline is dominated by, from left to right, the Cathedral, the Town Hall, the conical dome of the Victoria Coffee House and the tower of Lewis's. In the foreground are little streets of red brick terraces, a chapel (York Street), factories and a corner pub. BELOW: The tudor-style gables of Byway Road are typical of the houses put up on the outskirts of Leicester in the 1930s.

ABOVE LEFT: The Victorian mansions of Stoneygate started to disappear in the twentieth century. An early example of this process can be seen here — the block of flats on Knighton Park Road, built in the 1930s. RIGHT: The toy shop on the now largely vanished and lovingly remembered Charnwood Street. BELOW LEFT: Leicester, like other provincial cities, had many suburban cinemas: some have been demolished, some have been turned over to Bingo, and others have become factories, warehouses or amusement arcades. This one, the Regal on Havelock Street, is used for industry. RIGHT: Grattan's factory in Nelson Street was designed by Bedingfield and Grundy in 1932 for Goddard's Plate Powder and Polish firm. It is daringly art deco: much of the surface is glass supported by thin aluminium bars, and the brickwork is fittingly decorative. Though over fifty years old its self-conscious modernism is undiminished.

& SON

Hoggett
HOGGETT
HOGGETT
Son
HOGGETT
LIVERIES
W & A GIL

OPPOSITE ABOVE: The widening of Charles Street, taken from the intersection of Charles Street and Humberstone Gate, looking south. The east side of the road was maintained, and buildings on the west were demolished. The building on the left with plaster panels on the upper storey is still there to-day, as is the block next to it, everything else has now been demolished. High Street before completion of its widening at the turn of the century. BELOW: The east end by the corner of New Bond Street. The old and new street frontage on the right; left is the gentleman's outfitters, Hogget's, some early nineteenth century buildings that still survive and, in the distance, the Royal Arcade built by Stephens in 1877. ABOVE: The west end slightly earlier: unlike the east end, widening took place on the south and not the north side. Some of the buildings on the left (north) still stand, notably the Haunch of Venison. LEFT: Urban renewal at its best: the Rod Hackney partnership has brought new life to North Evington; the back of houses on St Saviour's Road. CENTRE: Lewis's shop (G. de C. Fraser, 1935). RIGHT: Elizabeth House, by John Middleton, forms a massive end-stop to Granby Street.

LEFT: Charles Street in 1985: Epic House to the left is the home of BBC Radio Leicester, the first local radio station in the country. The Supermarket in the ground floor was once, according to the *Guinness Book of Records*, the largest in the country. Most of the buildings to the left were built in the 1930s, while in the background there are 1960s high-rise blocks. RIGHT: The Lee Circle Car Park was one of the earliest multi-storey car parks to be built in Leicester. BELOW: The interior of the Haymarket Shopping Centre, built 1971–3. The architects were the Building Design Partnership. Its construction meant the demolition of the Bell Hotel, a building that, in its day, gave dignity to Humberstone Gate. The hint of scale promised by the exterior is never fulfilled inside.

ABOVE: The auction in the Welford Road cattle market: the functional pen, seats, scale and auctioneer's desk are all painted green. Though few people unassociated with farming ever visit the market, it still has an important function in a still quite rural county. BELOW: Two estate cottages: LEFT: Cressida Place, a terrace built for the Winstanleys by William Butterfield in 1859; RIGHT: semi-detached houses on Gooding Avenue designed by James Fyffe in 1928–32. It is remarkable how similar they are.

OPPOSITE ABOVE: Houses on the Braunstone Estate: the rural effect was in accord with the principles of the Garden Suburb movement. BELOW: The Winefred Street tenements were the first public housing in Leicester, built in 1900 by a private architect, T.H. Fosbrooke. ABOVE LEFT: Two different kinds of Council houses: detached houses of the 1920s on The Wayne Way, and Towers of the Rowlatts Hill Estates, which date from 1964 when Stephen George was City Architect. RIGHT: Leicester has two churches by Sir Basil Spence, architect of Coventry Cathedral: St High's, Eyres Monsell (1957) and this one: St Aidan's New Parks (1957). BELOW: The latest in Council Housing: Balderstone Drive is part of the second phase of the Rowlatt's Hill Estate, named after Chris Balderstone, a member of Leicestershire's victorious County Championship team of 1975.

LEFT: St John's Primary School on East Avenue was designed in 1971 by the Douglas Smith Stimson partnership. The section on the left is the hall; note the windows which are hung from a series of metal beams. At one time, Leicester had many church schools; now few remain. RIGHT: The Kimberlin Library and Exhibition hall, built between 1973 and 1977 in the fierce red brick made popular by Stirling's Engineering building in the University, is evidence of the rapid expansion of Leicester Polytechnic. Because the Polytechnic has always been closer to the City's heart (both geographically and emotionally) its buildings tend to be named after local men: Archibald Kimberlin was a Conservative Councillor for many years. BELOW: A feature of Leicester since the 1960s has been the development of large American-style shopping centres on the outskirts of the City. This one, Waitrose, is on Ethel Road; it comprises a large supermarket, some smaller shops and a public house. Behind is an attractive high-rise block and some good modern terraces. The shopping complex was designed by Anthony Drew-Edwards.

ABOVE: The new St Martin's development swept away most of a pleasantly quirky line of old buildings. CENTRE: Amadis Close is a secluded yet spacious Council development on Beaumont Leys. BELOW: The three violently contrasting towers of the University as they are seen from Welford Road: right, the explicitly mannerist Engineering Building by Stirling and Gowan (1959), centre, the Attenborough building like eighteen storeys of egg-boxes (Arup, 1968), and left, Sir Denys Lasdun's Charles Wilson building (1962) in sober exposed concrete. What will future generations make of them?

ABOVE: A shop window on Belgrave Road: figures such as these are one of the visual contributions the Asian community has made to Leicester shops. BELOW: Diwali is the chief festival of the Hindu population of Leicester. Each October the Council erect lights (Diwali is the festival of lights) along Belgrave Road. In fact, they are traditional Christmas decorations – stars and candles – but nobody seems to mind.

The Asian Contribution

Leicester has one of the highest Asian populations of any English city. Such a substantial and distinctive element cannot be overlooked, but from the viewpoint of the buildings of Leicester it present a problem. The Asian contribution to the City, though in many ways profound and far-reaching, is not one that has, as yet, expressed itself in an architecturally distinctive way. In fact, visually, it comes down to two things: shops and the re-use of buildings.

Asians who have come to Leicester in the last twenty years have tended to settle in specific areas. There are large numbers living in and around Belgrave Road and further east into Rushey Mead. There are also concentrations off the Humberstone Road, in and around North Evington and Green Lane Road, in Spinney Hill, St Saviours and Highfields. It is difficult to generalise but, roughly speaking, religion plays a part in residence: Belgrave tends to be Hindu, whereas North Evington is Muslim.

Belgrave is a good place to see Asian shops. The main road is now quite oriental. Most of the small shops bear Asian names – Karania, Lakhani, Patel. Their windows are brighter and more crowded than in many Leicester shops. The newsagents are particularly interesting. In the shop windows there are posters of Indian film stars, calendars, wall charts in both Gujarati and English, books with titles such as *Gujarati Self-taught* or *Learn Urdu in 30 Days* (Asian languages are increasingly spoken rather than written), religious bookmarks (the Asian equivalent of the kind of things found in a Catholic Repository) and bright, even gaudily coloured pictures of gods with their serene smiles and large brown eyes. Outside, street advertisements in Gujarati, Hindi or Punjabi stand on the pavement in place of ones inviting the passer-by to purchase ice-cream. The colours are not subtle and there seems little effort to 'display' goods in the English manner, yet the impression is one of life, vigour and commercial enterprise.

Even more oriental to the non-Asian population are the Saree shops. Specially made Indian models stand in the window with regally heaped up hair, large brown eyes and curving eyebrows. They are usually surrounded by sheets of material, often red, orange and yellow. Inside, Indian music plays and the salespeople and shoppers, with the exception of one or two English punks buying nose jewellery, are all Asian and speak Indian languages. The sarees themselves, being long lengths of material hemmed at both ends, are displayed, like curtain fabric, on circulating stands. The best silk ones are so fine they can be pulled with ease through a wedding ring.

There are also specialist jewellery shops, photographers that specialise in Asian style compositions, shops whose windows are piled high with huge, shining pans, tiny supermarkets emitting exotic smells and, of course, the wonderful Indian restaurants. The Indian restaurant is one of the areas (school, or course, is another) where east and west meet. If one talks to many Leicester residents, particularly the middle class, one finds that many have their favourite. This is not surprising. The food served on Belgrave Road is excellent, the service of a particularly high standard and the atmosphere open and friendly (I have been invited into the kitchen of one restaurant to see a clay oven – not something that has happened to me in Leicester's English restaurants). Those who own the restaurants are rightly proud of them. One (with justification) advertises itself as selling 'finest vegetarian dishes in Europe.'

There is one Belgrave Road institution which should be mentioned – the Natraj Cinema: a purpose-built Indian cinema which, at one time, was famous throughout the Midlands as a place of entertainment. It is plain and unobtrusive – concrete and brick – with nothing of the romance of the 1930s picture palaces but it is, or rather was spoken of with pride. The past tense is significant. The Asian community have embraced the video much more wholeheartedly than any other section of the community. The Asian video shop is now a feature of the townscape.

In the Asian communities, be they Hindu or Moslem, religion and social life are closely integrated. There is, therefore, a need for religious and community buildings. What has happened in Leicester is that shops, industrial premises and churches have been converted into temples, mosques and community centres. The Asfordby Street Mosque is the sometime canteen of Imperial Typewriters. It is an interesting building. Outside there are large notices, and inside a lobby where the faithful remove their shoes, and beyond some doors a vast worship space covered by an enormous carpet. With the exception of a large chair and a moorish shaped 'reredos' on the far wall, the building is impressively empty and thus eloquent of the unpicturable transcendence of Allah. The Belgrave Community Centre on Belgrave Road is the old Belgrave Hall Methodist Church, an 1898 building in nonconformist Baroque by Arthur Wakerley. It has a thoroughly secular not to say political air about it (a glance at the notice board tells you that), so there is a weird contrast between architecture and usage – an angel on the front and posters against the government within.

A more interesting and certainly more problematic contrast is provided by the sometime Carey Hall and the church of Our Lady, Moira Street, both of which are now Hindu temples. There is a degree of irony in the former. William Carey left Leicester for what was to be a most distinguished missionary career in India. The Baptist Church built in honour of him in 1897 by Redfern and Sawday was sold to Hindus in the early 1970s. It now has oriental panels within the windows and bears the name Shree Sanatan Mandir beneath a pediment of moulded brick and terracotta. It looks very Indian, but can such a building survive such a contradiction of intentions and uses? I assume that both the old and present owners think so. Our Lady, Moira Street was a small Roman Catholic church at the Harrison Road end of Moira Street. An image of Our Lady had been placed in a niche above the door – and she still stands there. Within, the floor is empty, and in the former sanctuary there glitter tiny, smiling goddesses, brightly clothed in red and swathed in thin gold thread. I just do not know what to make of such a clash of religious imagery.

The most interesting re-use is under way as this book goes to press. Leicester is to be established as a European centre for Jains. The Jains have bought Oxford Street Congregational Church, an 1865 building by Shenton and Baker, and they intend to clad it in marble. Work has started, but the process of transformation looks like being lengthy.

Yet the Jain Centre is not quite the latest move in the acquisition and re-use of religious buildings. The latest point of interest is a question: what will the Church of England do? A whole-sale campaign to declare redundant many of the inner city Victorian churches has begun. Will the Diocese of Leicester follow that of Portsmouth and sell to non-Christian faiths? It is an important question because, among other things, the visual future of Leicester depends upon it.

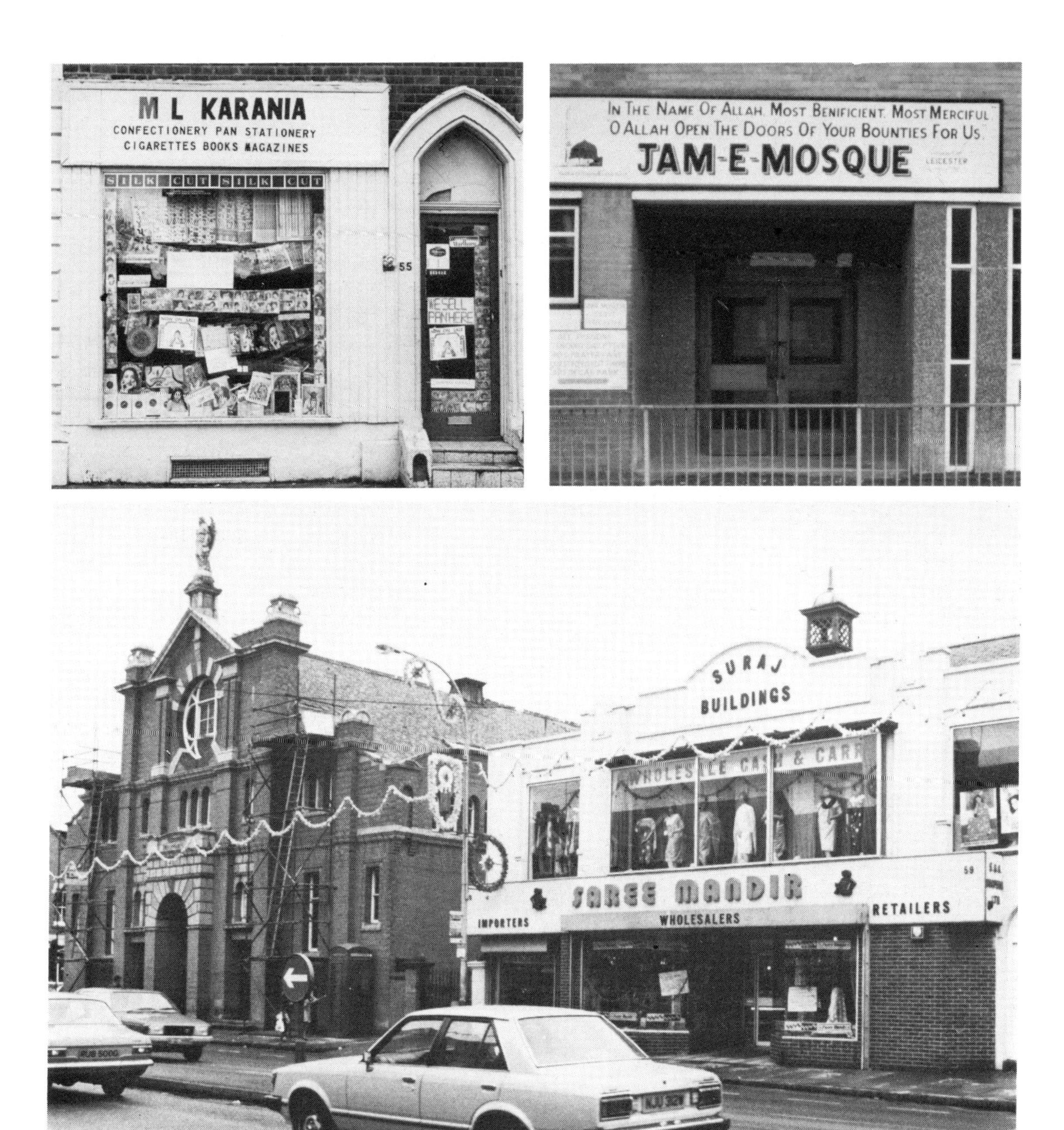

LEFT: M. L. Karania's shop on Belgrave Gate has a window packed with Indian goods: wall charts, bi-lingual readers, books on Indian languages and calendars. RIGHT: The Asfordby Street Mosque occupies what was once the canteen for Imperial Typewriters. BELOW: The Belgrave Hall was once a Methodist church; now it functions as a community centre in an area which is strongly Asian. Next door is one of the most interesting Saree shops: it must be a building of the 1920s or 1930s, but somehow the contents of its windows give the whole building an oriental look.

ABOVE: Our Lady's, Moira Street, is now a Hindu Temple. BELOW: William Carey left Leicester for a distinguished ministry in India. In his honour a Baptist Church, designed by Redfern and Sawday, was built in Catherine Street in 1897. It is now a Hindu temple.

Epilogue: the Character of Leicester

Leicester is a neglected provincial town. Surely even those locals who regard the Clock Tower as the hub of the universe are surprised to find it mentioned on the news. Not that it often is. Try sometime playing that undemanding parlour game 'Spot Leicester' when watching BBC's *Midlands Today*. Usually it is only crime that stirs the mandarins of Pebble Mill to take notice of us. Even worse is Midlands sport: it is not that Leicester wins, but that Aston Villa loses; and when, a few years ago, Leicester City won promotion to the first division by becoming second division champions, the headline from Pebble Mill was that Birmingham, who came second, were to go up! And if, more seriously, one turns to history, how many school text books on Roman Britain feature the Jewry Wall?

It must, however, be admitted that this neglect is not difficult to understand: Leicester has been marginal in English history. Richard III was brought here when dead; Wolsey came to die, and William Carey made Leicester famous by leaving it for India. Leicester, indeed, has had little luck; it is therefore a delightful paradox that author Sue Townsend, a resident of Leicester, should have been so successful with that typically Leicester resident – Adrian Mole. And it is perhaps significant that it is our University that is unique in establishing a Faculty of (sic) Local History. With the exception of the Jewry Wall, the Guildhall, the two Gimson houses and the Engineering building at the University, we have no buildings of national importance. And though in this century we have had our 'firsts', they are not spectacular: traffic wardens and the first – and very good – BBC Local Radio station. Its sporting successes have not quite been main-line: its soccer is shaky (City can never quite convince us that they are unmistakably first division), and its real success comes in Rugby (the Tigers are clearly the best English club of the last ten years) and, very recently, basketball. It has staged important boxing matches and now stages, at Saffron Lane, international cycling. And who outside Leicester appreciates the fact that in the last fifteen years Leicestershire has provided England with two cricket captains – Ray Illingworth and David Gower?

Yet towns can live without fame and spectacular success. What then does Leicester offer? My answer is modesty, variety, a gentle spaciousness and a winning domesticity.

Leicester is a modest, unassuming and accommodating place. Its buildings are often interesting, occasionally charming, sometimes good and even, in one or two cases, very good. But above all, they are rarely loud and trumpeting. At its best Leicester architecture is neither showy nor stridently self-conscious. Think of Gimson's White House, which is so faithful to vernacular traditions that people often assume that it is an old farmhouse, which has managed to survive into the twentieth century. Think again of the two circular libraries – St Barnabas and Southfields; neither shout and neither are showy. Think, above all, of our lovely Town Hall – so homely, so dignified without being daunting and so attractive without being either fussy or self-indulgent. It is a paradox, therefore, that our one world-famous building – the Engineering tower – is so deeply untypical of the City in which it stands. Stirling's daring building is striking and incurably self-regarding, whereas Leicester itself is unobtrusively modest.

But Leicester's modesty allows variety. The lively, individualistic spirit of the place has, with the exception of the housing estates, produced streets which are pleasingly bitty. A good example is King Street. On the corner with Wellington Street G.P.K. Young's black and white Tudor Office of 1930 would seem to herald a street of confident commercialism, yet what follows is: some delightful Victorian shops on the corner with New Walk (Stockdale Harrison 1888), the Civic Centre, a good Victorian factory by William Flint on the corner of Marlborough Street, a good early nineteenth century brick pub, a grey brick factory, through a gate Leicester's 'listed' slum – Crammant's yard – the Crescent, the stuccoed Crescent Cottages and, our best end-stop in Leicester, Holy Trinity. This variety is a reflection of the way the people of Leicester, have saved and spent: each person buys a small plot and builds on it in his or her own way.

And there was always land to buy. When it did grow, Leicester spread out gradually and evenly. There was never, as there was in Nottingham, dense overcrowding. Leicester's spaciousness was never grand and it was never at the expense of intimacy. The 'cosy' atmosphere celebrated and lamented in the last chapter was never claustrophobic. It is in the parks where this gentle spaciousness is mostly clearly experienced. From the big spaces of Western and Spinney Hill Park to the small recreation grounds on Fosse and Uppingham Roads, the immediate scale is human. The people who use them look at home and are never over-awed by either wildness or grandeur.

The parks, like the streets and houses, are winningly domestic. Leicester, it has often been said, is a town of red and green: the former the colours of brick, the latter of a nature that has been tamed but never banished. Leicester's houses at their most attractive – be they in Stoneygate or Beaumont Leys – are traditional. None are very large (the biggest were the Edwardian ones in Oadby), most are built in brick and refined by wood, tile or roughcast, and they stand in spaces which neither cramp nor imbue their owners with false illusions of grandeur. And because of the nature of the local industries, they are clean.

So Leicester is provincial, neglected, modest, varied, spacious and homely. Is there anything more to say? Only this: Leicester, though neither mysterious nor, upon first acquaintance, an exciting place, has interested and intrigued many newcomers who have got to know it. Three recent writers who have celebrated it most warmly – Malcolm Elliott, W.G. Hoskins and Jack Simmons – were all born and brought up elsewhere, and yet they found Leicester endearing, admirable and even delightful. In short, Leicester can arouse a deep affection in its citizens. And perhaps even more: there is a stronger emotion the strength of which would seem incompatible with a place as unassuming as Leicester, yet it would be wrong to deny that many have been surprised to find it aroused in them by this mild, provincial Midland City.

ABOVE: Two Leicester roof lines: the terrifying monster perches on an 1878 house by Stockdale Harrison, which was built for Mr Harvey, a solicitor, on the corner of New Walk and University Road (then called Victoria Road). The much more genial owl with his attendant moon can be seen on an early twentieth century house by Frank Seale at the London Road end of Holmfield Road. BELOW: Bradgate Street, laid out by the Leicester architect William Millican in 1872, was one of a little group of streets off Woodgate — Opal Street, the first on the left and, further up the road, Littleton Street, Diamond Street and Crystal Street. For many people streets like this were what made Leicester Leicester: safe, cheerful, familiar red brick houses set in straight streets lit by gas and served by useful corner shops.

Late Victorian doorways: here are four which survived untouched into the 1980s. The doorways can be found as follows: in ABOVE LEFT: Knighton Park Road; RIGHT: Princess Road; BELOW LEFT: St John's Road; RIGHT: Springfield Road.

LEFT: the country in the City: the west side of Stoneygate Avenue represents a late Victorian and Edwardian ideal; ample houses in distinctly traditional materials, all designed between 1898 and 1900 by Joseph Goddard's firm. RIGHT: New Walk in summer. BELOW: No area in Leicester was left untouched by the rapid re-development of the 1960s. Stoneygate suffered less than Victorian suburbs in other cities, largely because most of the houses were small enough to survive in an age without servants. Those that were demolished were usually replaced by flats; these ones are on the corner of Albert and London Roads.

LEFT: These attractive houses, built in 1894 in Springfield Road, were designed by Joseph Goddard of Goddard and Paget. RIGHT: In 1900 Walter Brand designed the wholesale fruit market, a good building with art nouveau decoration. When it was demolished, two luscious mermaids were saved, and in 1980 they were replaced by the West Bridge. Like the Turkey Café they were the work of Neatby of Doulton. BELOW: High Victorian summer in Spinney Hill Park: in the foreground is the stream which was sometimes dammed to form a pool for swimming; in the middle distance is one of the rural lodges designed by Stockdale Harrison, and to the right on the skyline is the oriental tower of the Imperial Hotel.

Index

Subscribers

Presentation Copies

1 Leicester City Council
2 Leicestershire County Council
3 Leicester University
4 Leicestershire Library Authority
5 Newarke Houses Museum
6 Vaughan College
7 Charles Phythian-Adams

8 Miss Margaret Evans
9 Richard & Mary Gill
10 Clive & Carolyn Birch
11 Eric Swift
12 Miriam Gill
13 Naomi Gill
14 Chris Dove
15 Peter M. Bone
16 Peter Spenlove-Spenlove
17 Mrs G. Sanders
18 Mrs J. Haywood
19 Alison M. Barradale
20 Hilary J. Smith
21 L.W. Jarvis
22 Annette Walia
23 Alan M. Joyce
24 J.P. Cunnington
25 S.M. Winder
26 Mary Danaher
27 Sybil Gamble
28 Brian Screaton
29 Hammerskey
30 Mrs D.R.W. Davidson
31 Eric Sanby
32 P. M. Le Bas
33, 34 L. R. Baker
35 M.J. Phillips
36 B.L. Leete
37 Christine Barry
38 Helen Knight
39 Victoria & Albert Museum
40 London Guildhall Library
41 Harold Thomas Walker
42 M. A. Cocks
43 B. L. Wright
44 M. J. Cufflin
45 Charles Craddock
46 Mrs Eileen Chambers
47 Lewis A. B. Lowe
48 Raymond Freestone
49 D. V. Ingleby
50 Robert Smyth School
51 T. P. Archer
52 Jennifer Macgregor
53 J. M. Spiers
54 J. C. Ault
55 J. A. Bull
56 S. M. F. Fraser
57 A. W. Stephenson
58 Leicestershire Archaeological and Historical Society
59 Miss J. M. Lee
60 M. B. Clark
61 Dr P. A. Kirkham
62 Mark E. Balding
63 Andrew W. King
64 Rowan Roenisch
65 T. Walton
66 Miss H. R. Whitbread
67 N. Burke-Bloor
68 Hugh Collinson
69 I. L. Dakin
70 R. J. Kitchen
71 Mrs J. Stevenson
72 Josephine M. Vivan
73 Mrs S. Symons
74 P. A. Neaverson
75 Philip Lindley
76 G. N. Lewitt
77
78 D. C. Edwards
79 J. R. Pepper
80 Joseph Hackney
81, 82 Joan E. Matthews
83 W. H. Brock
84 Roy Mackenzie
85 Mrs Daphne Machon
86 Paul Heron
87 Kenneth Woodfield
88, 89 David Thorpe
90 K. W. Sims
91 J. D. Swales
92 C. W. Hudson
93 Mrs B. Haselgrove
94, 95 R. A. Sanson
96 Audrey Dakin
97 Eileen Pinchbeck
98 John Crofts
99 Kerr's Displays Ltd
100 Dr. John F. Matthews
101 Mrs Mary Matthews
102 R. Emberton
103 Mrs Glennison Weston
104 Alan Kennedy
105, 106 T. Garield
107 Sheila M. Howland
108 T. H. Conway
109 Ian Metcalf
110 Allan Gort Measey
111 Ron Foster
112 Miss Marjorie Hole
113 Philip McNally
114 J. K. Pearson
115 Mr & Mrs G. Skipton
116 M. Fisher
117 Harry Rose
118 A. H. Jarvis
119 Mrs J. Ridgeway
120 Malcolm Elliott
121 Mrs J. Lytollis
122 Mrs. M. Orphen
123 Mrs Betty J. Wilson
124, 125 Mrs D. Buchan
126 Mrs M. T. Staunton
127 T. H. Harris
128 Dr. D. E. Drife
129 A. H. Willimas
130 N. Bush
131 J. Parker
132 C. M. Dunkley
133–176 Leicestershire Libraries & Information Service
177 Linda Hargreaves
178 Donald Percy
179 I. J. Hubbard
180 Miss G. N. Castledine
181 Mrs P. V. Wright
182 Mrs R. Needham
183 Mrs A. Smith
184 Mrs M. Parkin
185 Mrs P. L. Fisher
186 B. J. Smith
187 John W. Banner
188 Miss Kathleen Burton
189 Mrs Phyllis Berhan
190 F. J. Gallagher
191 Avenue Junior School
192 Mrs J. N. Nornel
193 Pam Baker
194 Mrs S. Fraser
195 Mrs Barbara Jones
196 Paul Hickinbotham
197 J. Leverka
198 M. Capenerhurst
199 N. F. Carter
200 R. M. Lupton
201 Dr. C. J. Dewey
202 K Donaldson
203 Mrs B. Salem
204 Mrs M. Turvey
205 David Moore
206 R. F. Taylor
207 Mrs M. Hillyard
208 Philip R. Goodwin
209 K. H. Wheatley
210 Mrs M. F. Sharp
211 Polly McLellan
212 D. Booth
213 F. H. Gulliver
214 Elizabeth Bond
215 Andrew & Ashwell
216, 217 Miss M. M. Gilbert
218 Jan Edward Zientek
219 R. A. McKinley
220 Yvonne Hayhurst
221 Dave Scott
222 Miss N. Waddington
223 C. Bent
224 Margaret Jean Downing
225 Nicholas M. Thompson
226 Richard Williamson
227 Helen V. Kinton
228 John Holt
229 Pamela F. Kilby
230 G. H. Jackson
231 Peter Johnson
232 R. H. & A. K. B. Evans
233 Sylvia Ann Radford
234 Nancy J. Herbert
235, 236 Leicester & County Chamber Of Commerce & Industry
237 John Garner
238 P. Whites
239 Mrs A. Marchant
240 J.W. Vincent
241 Mrs J. Bech
242 Dr A. D. McWhirr
243 D. R. Hayhurst
244 D. C.A.J. Macafee
245 C. Elliot
246 J.P. Ramsell
247 J.H.S. Nickson
248 P. Bailey
249 Dr. P.G.F. Swift
250 Miss B. Wells
251 Mrs S. Betts
252 Trevor Overton
253 Mrs. B. P. McAllen
254 Leonard Glover
255, 256 C. J. Perridge
257, 258 Mrs A. E. Kevern

259 R. S. Edwards
260 Sir Ernest Oliver
261
262 D. J. Vann
263
264 James Lord
265 Anne E. Lloyd
266 B. V. Hubbard
267 F. J. Stevens
268 Alan MacVicar
269 Mr & Mrs Coleman
270 J. Richard Fowler
272 Mrs D. Barradell
273 A. R. Barradell
274 William Henry Killner
275 Terry Smith
276 James Thawley
277 E. Harrold
278 Miss M. M. Gilbert
279
280 M. Kellet
281 David M. Gillman
282 P. M. Varman
283
284 R. T. Turner
285 Mrs B. L. Nichols
286 J. Hayman
287 Mr J. M. Smith
288 A. E. Ellis
289 C. E. V. Goodwin
290 Mrs A. E. Butlin
291 C. L. Chappell
292 I. McLellan
293 R. F. Wheeler
294 Mrs J. Saunders
295 Miss E. A. Wright
296 R. W. Rind
297 Edwin C. Bentham
298 C. H. F. Knight
299
300 Bryan O. Cooper
301
302 M. J. Griffin
303 V. A. Pantling
304 Mrs Audrey Thomas
305
306 Jonathon E. O. Wilshere ACIS LHG
307 The Misses E. M. & E. B. Tompkin
308 G. F. Tompkin
309 Mrs J. Hardwick
310 Margaret Watson
311 Bernard Cole
312 Mrs Norma Lee
313 Dennis Cuthbert
314 W. Elkington
315 Mrs Aileen Kinchington
316 Mrs Linda Harris
317 William Murden
318 Clayton Bros (Coaches) Ltd
319 Betty Branson
320 J. M. Widdowson
321 Andrew Goodman
322 P. L. Howells
323 D. Worth
324 P. Sorrell
325 L. Lloyd-Smith
326 S. J. Page
327 John McLauchlan
328
329 Penny Shepherd
330 J. D. Haigh
331 David B. Morton
332 F. Bailey
333 Miss F. I. Loke
334 Mrs K. Baxter
335
337 Richard Gill
338 Kitty Loakes
339
340 Mrs J. Dove
341
342 G. M. S. Dove
343 Mrs Ann Hinchliffe
344 Sally J. Reayer
345 Peter Cole
346 June Thompson
347 Jan Inchley
348 Keith John Bentley
349 Gillian Mary Carter
350 Michael L. Jones
351 Arnold Ashby
352
353 David Brunning
354 E. F. Curtis
355 Stephen Butt
356 Mrs Louise Smith
357 Derek L. Turnidge
358 Ann Jordon
359 E. Shenton
360 Miss J. R. Goddard
361
366 Dr M. E. Morton

Remaining names unlisted

Bibliography

A great deal of the material in this book, particularly that concerned with architects, is the result of my own researches in the Leicestershire Records Office. Most of it appears in print for the first time. The following is a list of the other books I have consulted.

Bennett, J.D. *Leicestershire Architects 1700–1850*, Leicester Museums, 1968.

Brandwood, Geoffrey K. *The Anglican Churches of Leicester*, Leicestershire Museums, 1983.

Broadfield, A. *Leicester As It Was, Hendon Publishing Company, 1972.*

Brown, A.E. (ed.) The Growth of Leicester, Leicester University Press, 1972.

Chinery, C.A. *Leicester Casle and The Newarke*, Leicestershire Museums, 1981.

Clark, David T.-D. & Simmons, Jack *Old Leicester*, The Leicestershire Archaeological and Historical Society, 1962.

Elliott, Malcolm *Victorian Leicester*, Phillimore, 1979.

Ellis, Colin D.B. *History in Leicester*, Recreational and Cultural Services Department, Leiceser, 1976.

Fielding Johnson, Mrs. T. *Glimpses of Ancient Leicester*, Clarke & Satchell, 1906.

Green, Susan E. & Wilshere, Jonathan *A Short History of Leicester's Markets and Fairs*, Leicester Research Services. 1973.

Hoskins, W.G. *Leicestershire*, Hodder & Stoughton 1957.

Liddle, Peter *Leicestershire Archaeology: The Recent State of Knowledge* vols. 1 & 2, Leicestershire Museums, 1982.

Lloyd-Smith L. & Keene, R.J.B. *1872–1972 The First Hundred Years of the Leicestershire and Rutland Society of Architects*, 1972.

Pevsner, Nikolaus & Williamson, Elizabeth *The Buildings of England: Leicestershire and Rutland*, Penguin, 2nd Edition, 1985.

Potts, Graham 'New Walk in the Nineteenth Century', *Transactions of the Leicestershire and Rutland Archaeological and Historical Society*, XLIV, 1968–9.

Simmons, Jack *Leicester Past and Present*, 2 Volumes, Eyre Methuen, 1974.

Skillington, Florence E. *The Plain Man's History of Leicester*, Edgar Backus, 1959.

Skillington, S.H. *The Newarke: its origins and associations*, Leicester Municipal School of Art Press, 1912.

Wacher, John *The Roman Towns of Britain*, Batsford, 1974.

Watts, Susannah, *A Walk through Leicester*, 1804, re-published by Leicester University Press. 1967.

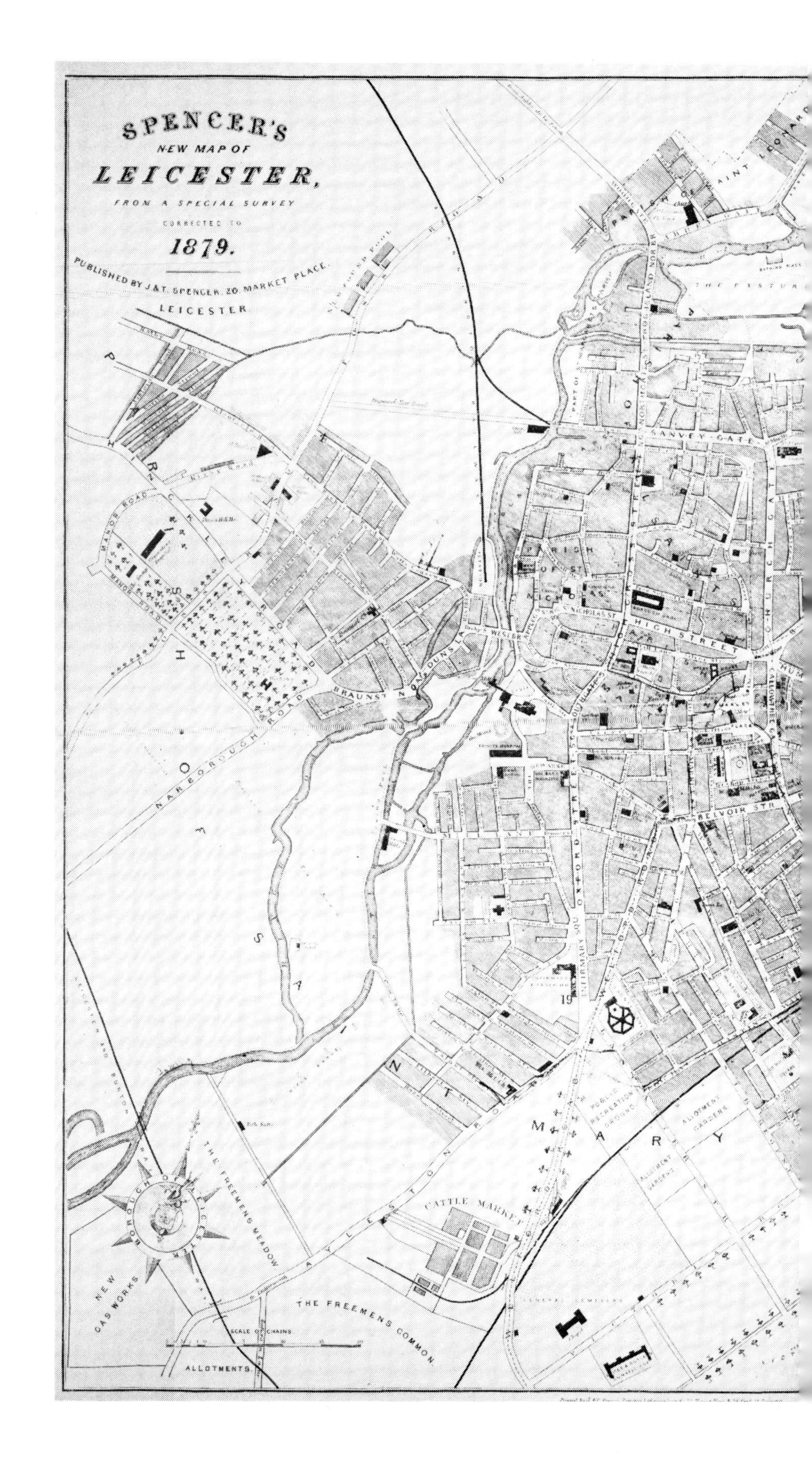
SPENCER'S
NEW MAP OF
LEICESTER,
FROM A SPECIAL SURVEY
CORRECTED TO
1879.
PUBLISHED BY J.&T. SPENCER, 20, MARKET PLACE,
LEICESTER.
SANVEY GATE
HIGH STREET
BELVOIR STR
NARBOROUGH ROAD
BRAUNSTONE GATE
MANOR ROAD
AYLESTON ROAD
WELFORD ROAD
OXFORD STREET
INFIRMARY SQU
CATTLE MARKET
PUBLIC RECREATION GROUND
ALLOTMENT GARDENS
THE FREEMENS MEADOW
THE FREEMENS COMMON
NEW GASWORKS
ALLOTMENTS
SCALE OF CHAINS
MARY
19